To:

Jesus said, "Let not your heart be troubled: ye believe in God, believe also in me."

JOHN 14:1

From:

GOD'S WORDS OF LIFE for

Women
of Color

from the King James Version

Compiled by
Snapdragon Editorial Group, Inc.

inspirio

GOD'S WORDS OF LIFE ON

GOD'S WORD OF LIFE ON

Jesus said, "My sheep hear my voice, and I know them, and they follow me: And I give unto them eternal life; and they shall never perish, neither shall any man pluck them out of my hand. My Father, which gave them me, is greater than all; and no man is able to pluck them out of my Father's hand."

John 10:27–29

God hath appointed a day, in the which he will judge the world in righteousness by Jesus Christ whom he hath ordained; whereof he hath given assurance unto all men, in that he hath raised him from the dead.

Acts 17:31

I the LORD thy God will hold thy right hand, saying unto thee, Fear not; I will help thee.

Isaiah 41:13

Jesus said, "Verily, verily, I say unto you, He that heareth my word, and believeth on him that sent me, hath everlasting life, and shall not come into condemnation; but is passed from death unto life."

John 5:24

GOD'S WORD OF LIFE ON
Assurance

The mountains shall depart, and the hills be removed; but my kindness shall not depart from thee, neither shall the covenant of my peace be removed, saith the LORD that hath mercy on thee.

Isaiah 54:10

Who shall separate us from the love of Christ? Shall tribulation, or distress, or persecution, or famine, or nakedness, or peril, or sword? ... Nay, in all these things we are more than conquerors through him that loved us. For I am persuaded, that neither death, nor life, nor angels, nor principalities, nor powers, nor things present, nor things to come, Nor height, nor depth, nor any other creature, shall be able to separate us from the love of God, which is in Christ Jesus our Lord.

Romans 8:35, 37–39

In God I will praise his word, in God I have put my trust; I will not fear what flesh can do unto me.

Psalm 56:4

GOD'S WORDS OF LIFE ON
Assurance

The work of righteousness shall be peace; and the effect of righteousness quietness and assurance for ever.

Isaiah 32:17

Be careful for nothing; but in every thing by prayer and supplication with thanksgiving let your requests be made known unto God. And the peace of God, which passeth all understanding, shall keep your hearts and minds through Christ Jesus.

Philippians 4:6–7

Nevertheless I am continually with thee: thou hast holden me by my right hand. Thou shalt guide me with thy counsel, and afterward receive me to glory. Whom have I in heaven but thee? and there is none upon earth that I desire beside thee. My flesh and my heart faileth: but God is the strength of my heart, and my portion for ever.

Psalm 73:23–26

Be still, and know that I am God: I will be exalted among the heathen, I will be exalted in the earth. The LORD of hosts is with us; the God of Jacob is our refuge.

Psalm 46:10–11

Humble yourselves ... under the mighty hand of God, that he may exalt you in due time: Casting all your care upon him; for he careth for you.
1 Peter 5:6–7

I know whom I have believed, and am persuaded that God is able to keep that which I have committed unto him against that day.

2 Timothy 1:12

Cast thy burden upon the LORD, and he shall sustain thee: he shall never suffer the righteous to be moved.

Psalm 55:22

Jesus said, "In the world ye shall have tribulation: but be of good cheer; I have overcome the world."
John 16:33

GOD'S WORDS OF LIFE ON
Assurance

*Fear was on every side ... But I trusted in thee, O
LORD: I said, Thou art my God.*

Psalm 31:13–14

*Jesus said, "Take no thought for your life, what ye
shall eat, or what ye shall drink; nor yet for your
body, what ye shall put on. Is not the life more
than meat, and the body than raiment? Behold
the fowls of the air: for they sow not, neither do
they reap, nor gather into barns; yet your heavenly Father feedeth them. Are ye not much better
than they? Which of you by taking thought can
add one cubit unto his stature? And why take ye
thought for raiment? Consider the lilies of the
field, how they grow; they toil not, neither do they
spin: And yet I say unto you, That even Solomon
in all his glory was not arrayed like one of these."*

Matthew 6:25–29

*I sought the LORD, and he heard me, and
delivered me from all my fears.*

Psalm 34:4

GOD'S WORD OF LIFE ON
Assurance

Delight thyself also in the LORD; and he shall give thee the desires of thine heart. Commit thy way unto the LORD; trust also in him; and he shall bring it to pass.

Psalm 37:4–5

Repent, and be baptized every one of you in the name of Jesus Christ for the remission of sins, and ye shall receive the gift of the Holy Ghost. For the promise is unto you, and to your children, and to all that are afar off, even as many as the LORD our God shall call.

Acts 2:38–39

For all the promises of God in him are yea, and in him Amen, unto the glory of God by us. Now he which stablisheth us with you in Christ, and hath anointed us, is God; Who hath also sealed us, and given the earnest of the Spirit in our hearts.

2 Corinthians 1:20–22

GOD'S WORDS OF LIFE ON
Assurance

As the heaven is high above the earth, so great is his mercy toward them that fear him. As far as the east is from the west, so far has he removed our transgressions from us.

Psalm 103:11–12

Jesus said, "For verily I say unto you, Till heaven and earth pass, one jot or one tittle shall in no wise pass from the law, till all be fulfilled. Whosoever therefore shall break one of these least commandments, and shall teach men so, he shall be called the least in the kingdom of heaven: but whosoever shall do and teach them, the same shall be called great in the kingdom of heaven."

Matthew 5:18–19

When thou liest down, thou shalt not be afraid; yea, thou shalt lie down, and thy sleep shall be sweet. Be not afraid of sudden fear, neither of the desolation of the wicked, when it cometh. For the LORD shall be thy confidence, and shall keep thy foot from being taken.

Proverbs 3:24–26

Making It
Home Safely
Reverend Dr. Alicia D. Byrd

I remember vividly the night I was followed home from the subway and attacked by an unidentified assailant. Deep in thought, I neglected to stay aware of my circumstances and to be on guard for unknown dangers. I thank God that I arrived home— shaken but unharmed. His protection and my training in self-defense enabled me to ward off my attacker.

In Proverbs 12:13, we read that the righteous person "shall come out of trouble." This means that when it seems like the river is about to overflow its banks, God's unseen hand will be your dam, preventing a flood from overwhelming you.

Even when you feel like Job, confused and wondering why every area of your life is under attack, hold on and give God the praise. Help is on the way. He promises to put a hedge around you and make a way for you in the midst of your trials and tribulations. Don't give up, but reach out to God. Say like the "old folks" said it, "Father, I stretch my hands to you, no other help I know."

The grace of our Lord was exceeding abundant with faith and love which is in Christ Jesus.

1 Timothy 1:14

Jesus said, "Blessed are the poor in spirit: for theirs is the kingdom of heaven. Blessed are they that mourn: for they shall be comforted. Blessed are the meek: for they shall inherit the earth. Blessed are they which do hunger and thirst after righteousness: for they shall be filled. Blessed are the merciful: for they shall obtain mercy. Blessed are the pure in heart: for they shall see God. Blessed are the peacemakers: for they shall be called the children of God. Blessed are they which are persecuted for righteousness' sake: for theirs is the kingdom of heaven."

Matthew 5:3–10

"I will make them and the places round about my hill a blessing; and I will cause the shower to come down in his season; there shall be showers of blessing," saith the LORD.

Ezekiel 34:26

We know that all things work together for good to them that love God, to them who are the called according to his purpose.

Romans 8:28

The LORD will give strength unto his people; the LORD will bless his people with peace.

Psalm 29:11

Thou, LORD, will bless the righteous; with favour wilt thou compass him as with a shield.

Psalm 5:12

Jesus said, "I am come that they might have life, and that they might have it more abundantly."

John 10:10

How excellent is thy lovingkindness, O God! Therefore the children of men put their trust under the shadow of thy wings. They shall be abundantly satisfied with the fatness of thy house; and thou shalt make them drink of the river of thy pleasures.

Psalm 36:7–8

GOD'S WORDS OF LIFE ON
Blessing

Blessed be the God and Father of our Lord Jesus Christ, who hath blessed us with all spiritual blessings in heavenly places in Christ.

Ephesians 1:3

Unto God that is able to do exceeding abundantly above all that we ask or think, according to the power that worketh in us, Unto him be glory in the church by Christ Jesus throughout all ages, world without end. Amen.

Ephesians 3:20–21

The meek shall inherit the earth; and shall delight themselves in the abundance of peace.

Psalm 37:11

Jesus said, "Whosoever hath, to him shall be given, and he shall have more abundance."

Matthew 13:12

Because the LORD thy God shall bless thee in all thine increase, and in all the works of thine hands, therefore thou shalt surely rejoice.

Deuteronomy 16:15

"The Blessings of God"

Reverend Dr. Charles Butler

Do you remember leaving home for the first time? As much as you may have longed for independence, you probably experienced the fear of the unknown as well.

Abraham had those same doubts and fears when God told him to leave home, family and everything familiar. He went forth believing that the God who promised blessings would honor his word and protect him on the journey. Abraham placed his confidence in God and learned that God's blessings followed him every step of the way.

Today, the Lord may ask you to separate yourself from those things that are safe and familiar and trust him to bless you. He may ask you to change jobs or remove yourself from a destructive relationship. You can be sure that whatever God asks of you, it is for your good. The journey of faith is not an easy one, but when you take God at his word, the growth, the blessings, the miracles are far greater than you could ever imagine. Stretch out and reach forward for all the blessings of God.

Behold, God is my salvation; I will trust, and not be afraid: for the LORD JEHOVAH is my strength and my song; he also is become my salvation. Therefore with joy shall ye draw water out of the wells of salvation. And in that day shall ye say, Praise the LORD, call upon his name, declare his doings among the people, make mention that his name is exalted. Sing unto the LORD; for he hath done excellent things: this is known in all the earth. Cry out and shout, thou inhabitant of Zion: for great is the Holy One of Israel in the midst of thee.

Isaiah 12:2–6

I will sing unto the LORD, for he hath triumphed gloriously. ... The LORD is my strength and song, and he is become my salvation: he is my God, and I will prepare him an habitation; my father's God, and I will exalt him.

Exodus 15:1–2

GOD'S WORD OF LIFE ON
Celebrate

Let them praise his name in the dance: let them
sing praises unto him with the timbrel and harp.
For the LORD taketh pleasure in his people: he
will beautify the meek with salvation.

Psalm 149:3–4

"Behold, I create new heavens and a new earth:
and the former shall not be remembered, nor
come into mind. Be ye glad and rejoice for ever in
that which I create: for, behold, I create Jerusalem
a rejoicing, and her people a joy. And I will
rejoice in Jerusalem, and joy in my people: and
the voice of weeping shall be no more heard in
her, nor the voice of crying," saith the Lord.

Isaiah 65:17–19

I have set the LORD always before me: because he
is at my right hand, I shall not be moved.
Therefore my heart is glad, and my glory
rejoiceth: my flesh also shall rest in hope.

Psalm 16:8–9

GOD'S WORDS OF LIFE ON
Celebrate

The ransomed of the LORD shall return, and come to Zion with songs and everlasting joy upon their heads: they shall obtain joy and gladness, and sorrow and sighing shall flee away.

Isaiah 35:10

God hast turned for me my mourning into dancing: God hast put off my sackcloth, and girded me with gladness; To the end that my glory may sing praise to him, and not be silent. O LORD my God, I will give thanks unto thee for ever.

Psalm 30:11–12

I will greatly rejoice in the LORD, my soul shall be joyful in my God; for he hath clothed me with the garments of salvation, he hath covered me with the robe of righteousness.

Isaiah 61:10

O clap your hands, all ye people; shout unto God with the voice of triumph. For the LORD ... is a great King over all the earth.

Psalm 47:1–2

A Cause for Celebration
Reverend Dr. Wilbur Daniel

On September 9, 1862, Abraham Lincoln signed the Emancipation Proclamation to free African slaves in America. Can you imagine the celebration as the word traveled from plantation to plantation, city to city, state to state? Stunned disbelief gave way to shouts of joy, hand clapping, and dancing. More than 200 years after the first African slave arrived in America, the institution of slavery was abolished.

The former African slaves could have focused on what they had endured. Instead, they gave praise to God who had blessed them with his deliverance.

As you reflect on your life, remember that you also have many causes for celebration. David names a few—forgiveness of sin, supernatural healing, redemption from destruction, and the execution of the righteous mercy of God (Psalm 103:3–6). God has richly blessed you.

Focus on all the things God has done for you. As you faithfully do his will, you will see his deliverance, and his blessings will continue to flow in your life.

GOD'S WORDS OF LIFE ON
Comfort

Yea, though I walk through the valley of the shadow of death, I will fear no evil: for thou art with me; thy rod and thy staff they comfort me.

Psalm 23:4

Blessed be God, even the Father of our Lord Jesus Christ, the Father of mercies, and the God of all comfort; Who comforteth us in all our tribulation, that we may be able to comfort them which are in any trouble, by the comfort wherewith we ourselves are comforted of God. As the sufferings of Christ abound in us, so our consolation also aboundeth by Christ.

2 Corinthians 1:3–5

The LORD is good, a strong hold in the day of trouble; and he knoweth them that trust in him.

Nahum 1:7

Though I walk in the midst of trouble, thou wilt revive me, O LORD: thou shalt stretch forth thine hand against the wrath of mine enemies, and thy right hand shall save me.

Psalm 138:7

GOD'S WORD OF LIFE ON
Comfort

*Jesus said, "If ye love me, keep my command-
ments. And I will pray the Father, and he shall
give you another Comforter, that he may abide
with you for ever."*

John 14:15–16

*Whatsoever things were written aforetime were
written for our learning, that we through
patience and comfort of the scriptures might
have hope.*

Romans 15:4

*I the LORD have called thee in righteousness, and
will hold thine hand, and will keep thee, and give
thee for a covenant of the people, for a light of the
Gentiles.*

Isaiah 42:6

*"As one whom his mother comforteth, so will I
comfort you,"… saith the Lord. And when ye see
this, your heart shall rejoice, and your bones shall
flourish like an herb: and the hand of the LORD
shall be known toward his servants . . . .*

Isaiah 66:13–14

GOD'S WORDS OF LIFE ON
Comfort

Jesus said, "The Comforter, which is the Holy Ghost, whom the Father will send in my name, he shall teach you all things, and bring all things to your remembrance, whatsoever I have said unto you."

John 14:26

The righteous cry, and the LORD heareth, and delivereth them out of all their troubles.

Psalm 34:17

The LORD, he it is that doth go before thee; he will be with thee, he will not fail thee, neither forsake thee: fear not, neither be dismayed.

Deuteronomy 31:8

God healeth the broken in heart, and bindeth up their wounds.

Psalm 147:3

Jesus said, "I will not leave you comfortless: I will come to you. Yet a little while, and the world seeth me no more; but ye see me: because I live, ye shall live also."

John 14:18–19

*I had fainted, unless I had believed to see the
goodness of the LORD in the land of the living.
Wait on the LORD: be of good courage, and he
shall strengthen thine heart: wait, I say, on
the LORD.*

Psalm 27:13–14

*Behold, the Lord God will come with strong
hand, and his arm shall rule for him: behold, his
reward is with him, and his work before him. He
shall feed his flock like a shepherd: he shall gather
the lambs with his arm, and carry them in his
bosom, and shall gently lead those that are
with young.*

Isaiah 40:10–11

*The LORD also will be a refuge for the oppressed,
a refuge in times of trouble.*

Psalm 9:9

*Let, I pray thee, O LORD, thy merciful kindness
be for my comfort, according to thy word unto
thy servant. Let thy tender mercies come unto me,
that I may live: for thy law is my delight.*

Psalm 119:76–77

Many are the afflictions of the righteous: but the LORD delivereth him out of them all.

Psalm 34:19

"When thou passest through the waters, I will be with thee; and through the rivers, they shall not overflow thee: when thou walkest through the fire, thou shalt not be burned; neither shall the flame kindle upon thee," saith the LORD.

Isaiah 43:2

Jesus said, "Blessed are you who hunger now, for you will be satisfied. Blessed are ye who weep now, for ye shall laugh."

Luke 6:21

Thus saith the high and lofty One that inhabiteth eternity, whose name is Holy; I dwell in the high and holy place, with him also that is of a contrite and humble spirit, to revive the spirit of the humble, and to revive the heart of the contrite ones.

Isaiah 57:15

I sought the LORD, and he heard me, and delivered me from all my fears.

Psalm 34:4

A God of Comfort
Reverend Dickerson L.S. Wells

History shows that many new-world settlers embraced strong religious convictions and lived by godly principles, which they instituted in America. The church had a far-reaching impact on the lives of the early settlers. Daily prayer and devotion were practiced in their homes, schools, and workplaces. God comforted them in their new home.

African Americans can boast of a similar history. Our ancestors possessed a strong faith that broke slavery's chains and eventually won freedom for our people. Through time they related their history and their faith in God to their children and to their children's children. God has comforted us as well.

But when we look at our communities, beset with violence, bloodshed, crime, battered family members, and many other problems, we must ask ourselves how far we have drifted away from God—away from his presence, his comfort, and his commands?

God is a God of comfort, but he is also a God of judgment. We must not forget our history. And we must not forget God.

GOD'S WORDS OF LIFE ON
Commitment

Said Jesus unto his disciples, "If any man will come after me, let him deny himself, and take up his cross, and follow me. For whosoever will save his life shall lose it: and whosoever will lose his life for my sake shall find it."

Matthew 16:24–25

Prove all things; hold fast that which is good. ... And the very God of peace sanctify you wholly; and I pray God your whole spirit and soul and body be preserved blameless unto the coming of our Lord Jesus Christ. Faithful is he that calleth you, who also will do it.

1 Thessalonians 5:21, 23–24

Look to yourselves, that we lose not those things which we have wrought, but that we receive a full reward. ... He that abideth in the doctrine of Christ, he hath both the Father and the Son.

2 John 8–9

Jesus said, "Whosoever heareth these sayings of mine, and doeth them, I will liken him unto a wise man, which built his house upon a rock: And the rain descended, and the floods came, and the winds blew, and beat upon that house; and it fell not: for it was founded upon a rock."

Matthew 7:24–25

Let us not be weary in well doing: for in due season we shall reap, if we faint not.

Galatians 6:9

Be obedient to them that are your masters . . . . Not with eyeservice, as menpleasers; but as the servants of Christ, doing the will of God from the heart; with good will doing service, as to the Lord, and not to men: knowing that whatsoever good thing any man doeth, the same shall he receive of the Lord.

Ephesians 6:5–8

Commit thy works unto the LORD, and thy thoughts shall be established.

Proverbs 16:3

GOD'S WORDS OF LIFE ON
Commitment

Delight thyself also in the LORD; and he shall give thee the desires of thine heart. Commit thy way unto the LORD; trust also in him; and he shall bring it to pass.

Psalm 37:4–5

Jesus said, "Behold, I come quickly: hold that fast which thou hast, that no man take thy crown. Him that overcometh will I make a pillar in the temple of my God, and he shall go no more out: and I will write upon him the name of my God, and the name of the city of my God, which is new Jerusalem, which cometh down out of heaven from my God: and I will write upon him my new name."

Revelation 3:11–12

Whoso looketh into the perfect law of liberty, and continueth therein, he being not a forgetful hearer, but a doer of the work, this man shall be blessed in his deed.

James 1:25

Commitment

True Caring and Commitment
Bishop Vinton Anderson

The biblical story of Naomi and Ruth makes a powerful statement about the power of commitment and surviving with dignity.

After the death of their husbands, Ruth declared her love and commitment to Naomi, her mother-in-law. Her willingness to remain single in order to care for Naomi demonstrated genuine sacrificial love.

While she performed the menial task of gathering leftovers, she attracted the attention of Boaz, who was a rich land owner, a relative of Naomi, and a truly altruistic person. Boaz showed great respect and concern for Ruth, and acknowledged her commitment to Naomi.

Faithfully fulfilling the law of the levirate, Boaz committed himself to redeem the family property and marry Ruth. Later, Ruth and Boaz had a son, Obed. The women of the community responded to this by saying, "Praise be to the LORD, who this day has not left you without a kinsman-redeemer" (Ruth 4:14).

What a glorious picture of God's commitment when he provided a kinsman-redeemer for us—his Son, Jesus Christ!

GOD'S WORDS OF LIFE ON
Courage

The LORD GOD will help me; therefore shall I not be confounded: therefore have I set my face like a flint, and I know that I shall not be ashamed.

Isaiah 50:7

Who is as the wise man? and who knoweth the interpretation of a thing? a man's wisdom maketh his face to shine, and the boldness of his face shall be changed.

Ecclesiastes 8:1

Be not afraid of sudden fear, neither of the desolation of the wicked, when it cometh. For the LORD shall be thy confidence, and shall keep thy foot from being taken.

Proverbs 3:25–26

The LORD is my strength and my shield; my heart trusted in him, and I am helped: therefore my heart greatly rejoiceth; and with my song will I praise him.

Psalm 28:7

GOD'S WORD OF LIFE ON
Courage

Be of good courage, and he shall strengthen your heart, all ye that hope in the LORD.

Psalm 31:24

Fear thou not; for I am with thee: be not dismayed; for I am thy God: I will strengthen thee; yea, I will help thee; yea, I will uphold thee with the right hand of my righteousness.

Isaiah 41:10

God wilt light my candle: the LORD my God will enlighten my darkness. By thee I have run through a troop; and by my God have I leaped over a wall.

Psalm 18:28–29

Be strong and of a good courage, fear not, nor be afraid: . . . for the LORD, thy God, he it is that doth go with thee; he will not fail thee, nor forsake thee.

Deuteronomy 31:6

What time I am afraid, I will trust in thee. In God I will praise his word, in God I have put my trust; I will not fear what flesh can do unto me.

Psalm 56:3–4

GOD'S WORDS OF LIFE ON
Courage

It is God that girdeth me with strength, and maketh my way perfect. He maketh my feet like hinds' feet, and setteth me upon my high places.

Psalm 18:32–33

When thou passest through the waters, I will be with thee; and through the rivers, they shall not overflow thee: when thou walkest through the fire, thou shalt not be burned; neither shall the flame kindle upon thee. For I am the LORD thy God, the Holy One of Israel, thy Saviour.

Isaiah 43:2–3

The LORD is my light and my salvation; whom shall I fear? The LORD is the strength of my life; of whom shall I be afraid? When the wicked, even mine enemies and my foes, came upon me to eat up my flesh, they stumbled and fell. Though an host should encamp against me, my heart shall not fear: though war should rise against me, in this will I be confident.

Psalm 27:1–3

Be Courageous
Bishop Cecil Bishop

A young man stands in the driveway looking back at the house where he has lived for the past eighteen years. Today marks the first day of a new chapter in his life—he is going to college.

College will open up new relationships, new challenges, new routines. How will he do? And what about his faith? Without his parents' faith to rely on, will he be true to God?

As Joshua faced the challenge of leading the children of Israel through the desert to the promised land, God reassured Joshua that he would not be alone. "Be strong and of good courage," said the Lord. "Don't let the possibility of failure paralyze you. Go forward, trusting in me, relying on me, keeping your eyes on me, and I will deliver you."

You, too, can choose to be courageous as you face new challenges. If your faith and confidence are in God, he will guide you through every circumstance.

Jesus said, "Blessed are you who hunger now, for you will be satisfied. Blessed are ye who weep now, for ye shall laugh."

Luke 6:21

Our Lord Jesus Christ himself, and God, even our Father, which hath loved us, and hath given us everlasting consolation and good hope through grace, Comfort your hearts, and stablish you in every good word and work.

2 Thessalonians 2:16–17

Jesus said, "These things I have spoken unto you, that in me ye might have peace. In the world ye shall have tribulation: but be of good cheer; I have overcome the world."

John 16:33

Why art thou cast down, O my soul? and why art thou disquieted within me? hope in God: for I shall yet praise him, who is the health of my countenance, and my God.

Psalm 43:5

[God's people] shall not labour in vain, nor bring forth for trouble; for they are the seed of the blessed of the LORD, and their offspring with them. And it shall come to pass, that before they call, I will answer; and while they are yet speaking, I will hear.

Isaiah 65:23–24

Then I said, I have laboured in vain, I have spent my strength for nought, and in vain: yet surely my judgment is with the LORD, and my work with my God.

Isaiah 49:4

This I recall to my mind, therefore have I hope. It is of the LORD's mercies that we are not consumed, because his compassions fail not. They are new every morning: great is thy faithfulness.

Lamentations 3:21–23

When I said, My foot slippeth; thy mercy, O LORD, held me up. In the multitude of my thoughts within me thy comforts delight my soul.

Psalm 94:18–19

Though our outward man perish, yet the inward man is renewed day by day. For our light affliction, which is but for a moment, worketh for us a far more exceeding and eternal weight of glory.

2 Corinthians 4:16–17

Jesus said, "Come unto me, all ye that labour and are heavy laden, and I will give you rest. Take my yoke upon you, and learn of me; for I am meek and lowly in heart: and ye shall find rest unto your souls."

Matthew 11: 28–29

Be ye strong, ... and let not your hands be weak: for your work shall be rewarded.

2 Chronicles 15:7

Then spake Jesus, saying, "I am the light of the world: he that followeth me shall not walk in darkness, but shall have the light of life."

John 8:12

The LORD is good unto them that wait for him, to the soul that seeketh him.

Lamentations 3:25

"All Other Ground is Sinking Sand"
Reverend Diane Hugger

Even the most faithful Christian can become discouraged, wondering if he or she has been forgotten by God. But Micah reminds us to look to God with faith. He says, "I will look unto the LORD; I will wait for the God of my salvation: my God will hear me" (Micah 7:7).

Even in times of discouragement, we are to be steadfast in our belief in God's compassion for his people. Micah prophesied, "Rejoice not against me, O mine enemy: when I fall, I shall arise; when I sit in darkness, the LORD shall be a light unto me" (Micah 7:8).

The words from an old familiar hymn express the confidence that we have in God and God alone:

> My hope is built on nothing less
> than Jesus' blood and righteousness.
> I dare not trust the sweetest frame,
> but wholly lean on Jesus' name.
> On Christ the solid rock I stand
> all other ground is sinking sand,
> all other ground is sinking sand.

Let your light so shine before men, that they may see your good works, and glorify your Father which is in heaven.

Matthew 5:16

Jesus said, "The gospel must ... be published among all nations. But when they shall lead you, and deliver you up, take no thought beforehand what ye shall speak, neither do ye premeditate: but whatsoever shall be given you in that hour, that speak ye: for it is not ye that speak, but the Holy Ghost."

Mark 13:10–11

Jesus said, "All power is given unto me in heaven and in earth. Go ye therefore, and teach all nations, baptizing them in the name of the Father, and of the Son, and of the Holy Ghost: Teaching them to observe all things whatsoever I have commanded you: and, lo, I am with you always, even unto the end of the world."

Matthew 28:18–20

These things command and teach. Let no man despise thy youth; but be thou an example of the believers, in word, in conversation, in charity, in spirit, in faith, in purity. Till I come, give attendance to reading, to exhortation, to doctrine. Neglect not the gift that is in thee, which was given thee by prophecy, . . . Meditate upon these things; give thyself wholly to them; that thy profiting may appear to all.

1 Timothy 4:11–15

God gave some, apostles; and some, prophets; and some, evangelists; and some, pastors and teachers; For the perfecting of the saints, for the work of the ministry, for the edifying of the body of Christ: Till we all come in the unity of the faith, and of the knowledge of the Son of God, unto a perfect man, unto the measure of the stature of the fulness of Christ.

Ephesians 4:11–13

God sent not his Son into the world to condemn the world; but that the world through him might be saved.

John 3:16–17

Jesus said, "When thou makest a dinner or a supper, call not thy friends, nor thy brethren, neither thy kinsmen, nor thy rich neighbours; lest they also bid thee again, and a recompence be made thee. But when thou makest a feast, call the poor, the maimed, the lame, the blind: And thou shalt be blessed; for they cannot recompense thee: for thou shalt be recompensed at the resurrection of the just."

Luke 14:12–14

Therefore if any man be in Christ, he is a new creature: old things are passed away; behold, all things are become new. All these things are of God, who hath reconciled us to himself by Jesus Christ, and hath given to us the ministry of reconciliation; To wit, that God was in Christ, reconciling the world unto himself, not imputing their trespasses unto them; and hath committed unto us the word of reconciliation.

2 Corinthians 5:17–19

I am not ashamed of the gospel of Christ: for it is the power of God unto salvation to every one that believeth.

Romans 1:16

Preaching the Good News

Reverend Dr. Ernestine Cleveland Reems

On January 1, 1863, President Abraham Lincoln signed the Emancipation Proclamation. On that great day the African slaves in America were declared officially free. More than 2000 years ago, Jesus declared another emancipation proclamation. "He hath sent me to bind up the broken hearted, to proclaim liberty to the captives, and the opening of the prison to them that are bound" (Isaiah 61:1; Luke 4:16).

Jesus, the Great Emancipator, came to free us from whatever binds, confines, entangles, or oppresses us and restore our joy so that we can praise and glorify him. And he has chosen every believer to be his witness. He has summoned us to invite others to accept salvation through Jesus Christ and preach the gospel of liberation and freedom.

Like the watchmen upon the walls of Jerusalem, we cannot help but speak the things that we have seen and heard because "the LORD has anointed [us] to preach good tidings" (Isaiah 61:1), the gospel of Jesus Christ.

We should be to the praise of God's glory, who first trusted in Christ. In whom ye also trusted, after that ye heard the word of truth, the gospel of your salvation: in whom also after that ye believed, ye were sealed with that holy Spirit of promise, Which is the earnest of our inheritance until the redemption of the purchased possession, unto the praise of his glory.

Ephesians 1:12–14

Whatsoever is born of God overcometh the world: and this is the victory that overcometh the world, even our faith. Who is he that overcometh the world, but he that believeth that Jesus is the Son of God?

1 John 5:4–5

Jesus said, "If ye have faith as a grain of mustard seed, ye shall say unto this mountain, Remove hence to yonder place; and it shall remove; and nothing shall be impossible unto you."

Matthew 17:20

They that know thy name will put their trust in thee: for thou, LORD, hast not forsaken them that seek thee.

Psalm 9:10

Jesus said, "Verily, verily, I say unto you, He that believeth on me, the works that I do shall he do also; and greater works than these shall he do; because I go unto my Father."

John 14:12

Be merciful unto me, O God, be merciful unto me: for my soul trusteth in thee: yea, in the shadow of thy wings will I make my refuge, until these calamities be overpast. I will cry unto God most high; unto God that performeth all things for me.

Psalm 57:1–2

Thou wilt keep him in perfect peace, whose mind is stayed on thee: because he trusteth in thee. Trust ye in the LORD for ever: for in the LORD JEHOVAH is everlasting strength:

Isaiah 26:3–4

GOD'S WORDS OF LIFE ON
Faith

Every word of God is pure: he is a shield unto them that put their trust in him.

Proverbs 30:5

As for God, his way is perfect: the word of the LORD is tried: he is a buckler to all those that trust in him.

Psalm 18:30

By grace are ye saved through faith; and that not of yourselves: it is the gift of God: Not of works, lest any man should boast.

Ephesians 2:8–9

Blessed is the man that trusteth in the LORD, and whose hope the LORD is.

Jeremiah 17:7

The fear of man bringeth a snare: but whoso putteth his trust in the LORD shall be safe.

Proverbs 29:25

Faith is the substance of things hoped for, the evidence of things not seen.

Hebrews 11:1

GOD'S WORD OF LIFE ON
Faith

The LORD is my strength and my shield; my heart trusted in him, and I am helped: therefore my heart greatly rejoiceth; and with my song will I praise him.

Psalm 28:7

They that trust in the LORD shall be as mount Zion, which cannot be removed, but abideth for ever.

Psalm 125:1

Without faith it is impossible to please God: for he that cometh to God must believe that he is, and that he is a rewarder of them that diligently seek him.

Hebrews 11:6

O taste and see that the LORD is good: blessed is the man that trusteth in him. O fear the LORD, ye his saints: for there is no want to them that fear him.

Psalm 34:8–9

GOD'S WORDS OF LIFE ON
Faith

*Being justified by faith, we have peace with God
through our Lord Jesus Christ: By whom also we
have access by faith into this grace wherein we
stand, and rejoice in hope of the glory of God.*

Romans 5:1–2

Whoso trusteth in the LORD, happy is he.

Proverbs 16:20

*He that trusteth in his own heart is a fool: but
whoso walketh wisely, he shall be delivered.*

Proverbs 28:26

*Judge me, O LORD; for I have walked in mine
integrity: I have trusted also in the LORD; therefore I shall not slide.*

Psalm 26:1

*The salvation of the righteous is of the LORD: he
is their strength in the time of trouble. The LORD
shall help them, and deliver them: he shall deliver
them from the wicked, and save them, because
they trust in him.*

Psalm 37:39–40

Faith in Action
Reverend Dr. Dandridge C. Wilborn

By faith, Moses "refused to be called the son of Pharaoh's daughter" (Hebrews 11:24). Instead, he became an active voice against the oppression, exploitation and sin of Egypt. By faith, Moses was able to see the invisible, eternal kingdom of God that rests on the foundation of justice and righteousness.

If our faith is a reality, we must relate the will of God to the affairs of this world. Fellowship with God carries with it this responsibility and makes his inexhaustible resources available to us.

By faith, we can be agents of redemption in our community. Our faith lived out individually and communally will ultimately help people conform more closely to God's will. One of those tasks is to give hope to those who are broken and battered by sin—to those who do not enjoy fellowship with our gracious God. If our faith is concentrated on eternal goals rather than temporal goals, we will be able to accomplish God's work in the world.

GOD'S WORDS OF LIFE ON
Family

I bow my knees unto the Father of our Lord Jesus Christ, of whom the whole family in heaven and earth is named, That he would grant you, according to the riches of his glory, to be strengthened with might by his Spirit in the inner man.

Ephesians 3:14–16

Behold, what manner of love the Father hath bestowed upon us, that we should be called the sons of God: therefore the world knoweth us not, because it knew him not. Beloved, now are we the sons of God, and it doth not yet appear what we shall be: but we know that, when he shall appear, we shall be like him; for we shall see him as he is.

1 John 3:1–2

A father of the fatherless, and a judge of the widows, is God in his holy habitation

Psalm 68:5

GOD'S WORD OF LIFE ON
Family

*God setteth the poor on high from affliction, and
maketh him families like a flock. The righteous
shall see it, and rejoice: and all iniquity shall stop
her mouth. Whoso is wise, and will observe these
things, even they shall understand the lovingkindness of the LORD.*

Psalm 107:41–43

*The living, the living, he shall praise thee, Lord,
as I do this day: the father to the children shall
make known thy truth.*

Isaiah 38:19

*Jesus took not on him the nature of angels; but he
took on him the seed of Abraham. Wherefore in
all things it behooved him to be made like unto
his brethren, that he might be a merciful and
faithful high priest in things pertaining to God, to
make reconciliation for the sins of the people. For
in that he himself hath suffered being tempted, he
is able to succour them that are tempted.*

Hebrews 2:16–18

GOD'S WORDS OF LIFE ON
Family

I will receive you, and will be a Father unto you, and ye shall be my sons and daughters, saith the Lord Almighty.

2 Corinthians 6:17–18

Thou shalt keep ... God's statutes, and his commandments, ... that it may go well with thee, and with thy children after thee, and that thou mayest prolong thy days upon the earth, which the LORD thy God giveth thee, for ever.

Deuteronomy 4:40

All thy children shall be taught of the LORD; and great shall be the peace of thy children.

Isaiah 54:13

Correct thy son, and he shall give thee rest; yea, he shall give delight unto thy soul.

Proverbs 29:17

Jesus called a little child unto him, and set him in the midst of them, ... [and] Jesus said, "Whosoever therefore shall humble himself as this little child, the same is greatest in the kingdom of heaven."

Matthew 18:2, 4

The LORD thy God will make thee plenteous in every work of thine hand, in the fruit of thy body, … and in the fruit of thy land, for good: for the LORD will again rejoice over thee for good, as he rejoiced over thy fathers.

Deuteronomy 30:9

Behold, how good and how pleasant it is for brethren to dwell together in unity!

Psalm 133:1

Fathers, provoke not your children to wrath: but bring them up in the nurture and admonition of the Lord.

Ephesians 6:4

Train up a child in the way he should go: and when he is old, he will not depart from it.

Proverbs 22:6

Children are an heritage of the LORD and the fruit of the womb is his reward. As arrows are in the hand of a mighty man; so are children of the youth. Happy is the man that hath his quiver full of them.

Psalm 127:3–5

God's Words of Life on
Family

God will love thee, and bless thee, and multiply thee: he will also bless the fruit of thy womb, and the fruit of thy land.

Deuteronomy 7:13

Children's children are the crown of old men; and the glory of children are their fathers.

Proverbs 17:6

Children, obey your parents in the Lord: for this is right. Honour thy father and mother; which is the first commandment with promise; That it may be well with thee, and thou mayest live long on the earth.

Ephesians 6:1–3

Blessed is every one that feareth the Lord; that walketh in his ways. For thou shalt eat the labour of thine hands: happy shalt thou be, and it shall be well with thee. Thy wife shall be as a fruitful vine by the sides of thine house: thy children like olive plants round about thy table.

Psalm 128:1–3

Remembering Our History

Reverend Dr. Dezo McGill

History has taught us that our destiny is not a matter of chance but choice. An uncertain future demands that we look to the past to gain a proper perspective for the present and joy for the journey of life ahead of us.

As African Americans we cannot deny our heritage and still remain focused on our common future. The mystery, the marvel, the challenge and the romance of Africa can inspire us to become change agents in our distressed communities.

To that end, we must resurrect the principle of the extended family if our children are expected to assume their rightful place in this world. We must nurture a healthy sense of self-esteem in each of them. We must further tell our children that our ancestors worshipped the one true God even before God's name was revealed to them. By doing these things we will help them get past the past and ensure for them a prosperous future.

Who is a God like unto thee, that pardoneth iniquity, and passeth by the transgression of the remnant of his heritage? He retaineth not his anger for ever, because he delighteth in mercy.

Micah 7:18

If we confess our sins, God is faithful and just to forgive us our sins, and to cleanse us from all unrighteousness.

1 John 1:9

"I, even I, am he that blotteth out thy transgressions for mine own sake, and will not remember thy sins," saith the LORD.

Isaiah 43:25

Jesus said, "If ye forgive men their trespasses, your heavenly Father will also forgive you."

Matthew 6:14

Come now, and let us reason together, saith the LORD: though your sins be as scarlet, they shall be as white as snow; though they be red like crimson, they shall be as wool.

Isaiah 1:18

You, being dead in your sins and the uncircumcision of your flesh, hath God quickened together with Christ, having forgiven you all trespasses; blotting out the handwriting of ordinances that was against us, which was contrary to us, and took it out of the way, nailing it to his cross.

Colossians 2:13–14

"I will cleanse them from all their iniquity, whereby they have sinned against me; and I will pardon all their iniquities, whereby they have sinned, and whereby they have transgressed against me," saith the Lord.

Jeremiah 33:8

Thou, Lord, art good, and ready to forgive; and plenteous in mercy unto all them that call upon thee.

Psalm 86:5

Judge not, and ye shall not be judged: condemn not, and ye shall not be condemned: forgive, and ye shall be forgiven.

Luke 6:37

To the praise of the glory of his grace, wherein he hath made us accepted in the beloved. In whom we have redemption through his blood, the forgiveness of sins, according to the riches of his grace; Wherein he hath abounded toward us in all wisdom and prudence.

Ephesians 1:6–8

Therefore if any man be in Christ, he is a new creature: old things are passed away; behold, all things are become new. All these things are of God, who hath reconciled us to himself by Jesus Christ, and hath given to us the ministry of reconciliation; To wit, that God was in Christ, reconciling the world unto himself, not imputing their trespasses unto them; and hath committed unto us the word of reconciliation.

2 Corinthians 5:17–19

Be ye kind one to another, tenderhearted, forgiving one another, even as God for Christ's sake hath forgiven you.

Ephesians 4:32

Henry's Story
Dr. Willie T. Snead

When Jesus gave his disciples a model for prayer, it included the notion of forgiveness: "Forgive us our trespasses as we forgive . . ." To the degree we forgive others, God will forgive us. If we don't forgive, God will not forgive us.

Each of us needs to look in the mirror and ask God to change our ways. Are there hurts we have not forgiven? Are there those we have refused to reconcile with? Is unforgiveness driving us to act in ways that are unpleasing to God?

We can experience the joy of letting go of our anger. We can be liberated from the desire to act in ways that harm rather than heal. Forgiveness benefits the other person, but it does even more for us. For as long as we harbor ill will toward others, we block our own spiritual growth, spiritual blessings, and usefulness to God. Ask God to give you a loving, reconciling heart today.

GOD'S WORDS OF LIFE ON
Generosity

He which soweth sparingly shall reap also sparingly; and he which soweth bountifully shall reap also bountifully. Every man according as he purposeth in his heart, so let him give; not grudgingly, or of necessity: for God loveth a cheerful giver.

2 Corinthians 9:6–7

Jesus said, "Give, and it shall be given unto you; good measure, pressed down, and shaken together, and running over, shall men give into your bosom. For with the same measure that ye mete withal it shall be measured to you again."

Luke 6:38

He that giveth unto the poor shall not lack.

Proverbs 28:27

A good man showeth favour, and lendeth: he will guide his affairs with discretion. Surely he shall not be moved for ever: the righteous shall be in everlasting remembrance.

Psalm 112:5–6

He that hath a bountiful eye shall be blessed; for he giveth of his bread to the poor.

Proverbs 22:9

Charge them that are rich in this world, that they be not highminded, nor trust in uncertain riches, but in the living God, who giveth us richly all things to enjoy.

1 Timothy 6:17

It is more blessed to give than to receive.

Acts 20:35

Jesus said, "Whosoever shall give you a cup of water to drink in my name, because ye belong to Christ, verily I say unto you, he shall not lose his reward."

Mark 9:41

Be not forgetful to entertain strangers: for thereby some have entertained angels unawares.

Hebrews 13:2

GOD'S WORDS OF LIFE ON
Generosity

Is not this the fast that I have chosen? ... Is it not to deal thy bread to the hungry, and that thou bring the poor that are cast out to thy house? when thou seest the naked, that thou cover him; and that thou hide not thyself from thine own flesh? Then shall thy light break forth as the morning, and thine health shall spring forth speedily: and thy righteousness shall go before thee; and the glory of the LORD shall be thy reward.

Isaiah 58:6–8

Jesus said, "He that receiveth you receiveth me, and he that receiveth me receiveth him that sent me. He that receiveth a prophet in the name of a prophet shall receive a prophet's reward; and he that receiveth a righteous man in the name of a righteous man shall receive a righteous man's reward. And whosoever shall give to drink unto one of these little ones a cup of cold water only in the name of a disciple, verily I say unto you, he shall in no wise lose his reward."

Matthew 10:40–42

Enough Is Plenty
The Honorable Floyd H. Flake

God calls the church to manifest his generosity. Yet we have often failed him by failing to heed his call to be stewards of all that he created. This is best seen in the line that separates the rich from the poor.

The love of money has created a world where godliness has become secondary to other pursuits. But God did not intend great gain for some and perpetual poverty for others. God's people must hear his call to replenish the earth, contribute to the development of communities, rebuild the broken structures of society, and reinvest their faith so that all the world might witness God's presence and power in a tangible way.

It is also our responsibility to develop a just stewardship of our own resources: to give with a cheerful attitude, lend to those who have need, learn how to live with peace of mind, whether we have money or not; and learn to rejoice in the wonderful blessings that God makes available to us.

Jesus said, "Where two or three are gathered together in my name, there am I in the midst of them."

Matthew 18:20

God that made the world and all things therein, seeing that he is Lord of heaven and earth, dwelleth not in temples made with hands; Neither is worshipped with men's hands, as though he needed any thing, seeing he giveth to all life, and breath, and all things; And hath made of one blood all nations of men for to dwell on all the face of the earth, and hath determined the times before appointed, and the bounds of their habitation; That they should seek the Lord, if haply they might feel after him, and find him, though he be not far from every one of us: For in him we live, and move, and have our being.

Acts 17:24–28

GOD'S WORD OF LIFE ON
God's Presence

*Yea, though I walk through the valley of the
shadow of death, I will fear no evil: for thou art
with me, O LORD.*

Psalm 23:4

*Be strong and of a good courage, fear not, nor be
afraid: ... for the LORD thy God, he it is that doth
go with thee; he will not fail thee, nor forsake
thee.*

Deuteronomy 31:6

*Jesus spake, saying, "Lo, I am with you always,
even unto the end of the world."*

Matthew 28:20

*The LORD is nigh unto all them that call upon
him, to all that call upon him in truth.*

Psalm 145:18

*Jesus said, "I will pray the Father, and he shall
give you another Comforter, that he may abide
with you for ever; Even the Spirit of truth; whom
the world cannot receive, because it seeth him not,
neither knoweth him: but ye know him; for he
dwelleth with you, and shall be in you."*

John 14:16–17

GOD'S WORDS OF LIFE ON
God's Presence

*O LORD, thou hast searched me, and known me.
... If I take the wings of the morning, and dwell
in the uttermost part of the sea; even there shall
thy hand lead me, and thy right hand shall hold
me.*

Psalm 139:1, 9–10

*"When thou passest through the waters, I will be
with thee; and through the rivers, they shall not
overflow thee: when thou walkest through the
fire, thou shalt not be burned; neither shall the
flame kindle upon thee," saith the LORD.*

Isaiah 43:2–3

*God said, My presence shall go with thee, and I
will give thee rest.*

Exodus 33:14

*If the Spirit of him that raised up Jesus from the
dead dwell in you, he that raised up Christ from
the dead shall also quicken your mortal bodies by
his Spirit that dwelleth in you.*

Romans 8:11

Up Close and Personal
Bishop J. Clinton Hoggard

After years of working for the release of Nelson Mandela in South Africa, I was excited to see him in person—out of prison and on free soil. The man we met was humble, articulate, charismatic, and intelligent—commanding great respect and loyalty. Seeing him face to face helped us comprehend who he was.

The incarnation of Jesus allowed us to experience God "up close and personal." Through his human presence, we saw how God loved his enemies, showed compassion for the hungry, sorrowed over a sinner who would not repent. Because Jesus came and sent "another Comforter" (John 14:16), we are able to experience God's love and presence through the Holy Spirit even now, a continuous and indwelling reminder of the person and nature of God.

No longer unseen, the Spirit of God comes "up close and personal" to all who will open their hearts, minds, and spirits and receive him as Lord and Savior.

In the beginning was the Word, and the Word was with God, and the Word was God. The same was in the beginning with God. All things were made by him; and without him was not any thing made that was made. In him was life; and the life was the light of men.

John 1:1–4

Jesus said, "It is written, Man shall not live by bread alone, but by every word that proceedeth out of the mouth of God."

Matthew 4:4

Blessed are they that hear the word of God, and keep it.

Luke 11:28

O how love I thy law! It is my meditation all the day. Thou through thy commandments hast made me wiser than mine enemies: for they are ever with me. I have more understanding than all my teachers: for thy testimonies are my meditation.

Psalm 119:97–99

GOD'S WORD OF LIFE ON
God's Word

Let the word of Christ dwell in you richly in all wisdom; teaching and admonishing one another in psalms and hymns and spiritual songs, singing with grace in your hearts to the Lord.

Colossians 3:16

Thy words were found, and I did eat them; and thy word was unto me the joy and rejoicing of mine heart: for I am called by thy name, O LORD God of hosts.

Jeremiah 15:16

Thy word is a lamp unto my feet, and a light unto my path, O LORD.

Psalm 119:105

Great peace have they which love thy law, O LORD: and nothing shall offend them.

Psalm 119:165

Study to show thyself approved unto God, a workman that needeth not to be ashamed, rightly dividing the word of truth.

2 Timothy 2:15

GOD'S WORDS OF LIFE ON
God's Word

All scripture is given by inspiration of God, and is profitable for doctrine, for reproof, for correction, for instruction in righteousness: that the man of God may be perfect, thoroughly furnished unto all good works.

2 Timothy 3:16–17

Thy testimonies are wonderful, O LORD: therefore doth my soul keep them. The entrance of thy words giveth light; it giveth understanding unto the simple.

Psalm 119:129–130

The word of God is quick, and powerful, and sharper than any twoedged sword, piercing even to the dividing asunder of soul and spirit, and of the joints and marrow, and is a discerner of the thoughts and intents of the heart.

Hebrews 4:12

Jesus said, "Heaven and earth shall pass away: but my words shall not pass away."

Mark 13:31

The Word Is Life
Reverend C. Dennis Edwards

Do you know someone who has every reason to be depressed and sullen but is instead perpetually joyful and full of life? Perhaps that person is imprisoned in a body ravished by disease or deteriorated by injury. Or he or she may have endured family turmoil, economic hardship, or personal misfortune. Yet, in spite of his or her circumstances, is thriving.

The secret of this authentic victorious living is found in Psalm 1. A life of unfailing joy grows when we are rooted in the Word of God (v. 2). Jesus said, "The words that I speak unto you, they are spirit, and they are life" (John 6:63).

In the Word of God, one can find renewed joy, renewed hope, renewed peace, renewed contentment, renewed strength, and a renewed passion for life. God's Word is a deep well and a refreshing stream. The person whose life is planted like a tree by this "stream of water" shall be constantly revitalized and motivated.

The kindness and love of God our Saviour toward man appeared, Not by works of righteousness which we have done, but according to his mercy he saved us, by the washing of regeneration, and renewing of the Holy Ghost; Which he shed on us abundantly through Jesus Christ our Saviour; That being justified by his grace, we should be made heirs according to the hope of eternal life.

Titus 3:4–7

Unto every one of us is given grace according to the measure of the gift of Christ.

Ephesians 4:7

By grace are ye saved through faith; and that not of yourselves: it is the gift of God: not of works, lest any man should boast.

Ephesians 2:8–9

John bare witness of him, and cried, saying… He that cometh after me is preferred before me: for he was before me. And of his fulness have all we received, and grace for grace. For the law was given by Moses, but grace and truth came by Jesus Christ.

John 1:15–17

GOD'S WORD OF LIFE ON
Grace

All have sinned, and come short of the glory of God; Being justified freely by his grace through the redemption that is in Christ Jesus: Whom God hath set forth to be a propitiation through faith in his blood, to declare his righteousness for the remission of sins that are past, through the forbearance of God; To declare, I say, at this time his righteousness: that he might be just, and the justifier of him which believeth in Jesus.

Romans 3:23–26

Jesus said, "My grace is sufficient for thee: for my strength is made perfect in weakness."

2 Corinthians 12:9

Grace and peace be multiplied unto you through the knowledge of God, and of Jesus our Lord.

2 Peter 1:2

Ye know the grace of our Lord Jesus Christ, that, though he was rich, yet for your sakes he became poor, that ye through his poverty might be rich.

2 Corinthians 8:9

GOD'S WORDS OF LIFE ON
Grace

The God of all grace, who hath called us unto his eternal glory by Christ Jesus, after that ye have suffered a while, make you perfect, stablish, strengthen, settle you.

1 Peter 5:10

I thank my God always on your behalf, for the grace of God which is given you by Jesus Christ; That in every thing ye are enriched by him, in all utterance, and in all knowledge.

1 Corinthians 1:4–5

God, who is rich in mercy, for his great love wherewith he loved us, Even when we were dead in sins, hath quickened us together with Christ, (by grace ye are saved;) and hath raised us up together, and made us sit together in heavenly places in Christ Jesus: That in the ages to come he might show the exceeding riches of his grace in his kindness toward us through Christ Jesus.

Ephesians 2:4–7

More Than Sufficient Grace

Dr. Horace C. Walser

In Christian usage, grace expresses one of the church's most distinctive and important doctrines. Paul's personal religious awakening produced in him an understanding of this extraordinary gift of God. Conscious of his guilt and unworthiness, Paul realized God's gift of forgiveness was a totally undeserved blessing. So he used the word grace to express his new-found understanding of the nature of God. Grace is the expression of the essence of God, whose very being is love.

God's grace enables us to bear what we could not otherwise bear and do what we could not otherwise do. Let this truth remind us to heed the biblical admonition to "grow in grace" (2 Peter 3:18).

We are to grow until we overcome self-centeredness; we are to grow in grace until our problems seem as though they were nothing in the light of God's love. To grow in grace means that we perceive that God is greater than anything that we might face in this world.

GOD'S WORDS OF LIFE ON
Guidance

*Trust in the LORD with all thine heart; and lean
not unto thine own understanding. In all thy
ways acknowledge him, and he shall direct
thy paths.*

Proverbs 3:5–6

*The LORD shall guide thee continually, and satis-
fy thy soul in drought, and make fat thy bones:
and thou shalt be like a watered garden, and like
a spring of water, whose waters fail not.*

Isaiah 58:11

*Jesus said, "When he, the Spirit of truth, is come,
he will guide you into all truth: for he shall not
speak of himself; but whatsoever he shall hear,
that shall he speak: and he will show you things
to come."*

John 16:13

*The LORD is my shepherd; I shall not want. He
maketh me to lie down in green pastures: he leadeth me beside the still waters. He restoreth my
soul: he leadeth me in the paths of righteousness
for his name's sake.*

Psalm 23:1–3

GOD'S WORD OF LIFE ON
Guidance

*Keep thy father's commandment, and forsake not
the law of thy mother: Bind them continually
upon thine heart, and tie them about thy neck.
When thou goest, it shall lead thee; when thou
sleepest, it shall keep thee; and when thou awak-
est, it shall talk with thee.*

Proverbs 6:20—22

*"I will instruct thee and teach thee in the way
which thou shalt go: I will guide thee with mine
eye," saith the Lord.*

Psalm 32:8

*Thou art my rock and my fortress; therefore for
thy name's sake lead me, and guide me, O LORD.*

Psalm 31:3

*Thus saith the LORD, thy Redeemer, the Holy
One of Israel; I am the LORD thy God which teacheth thee to profit, which leadeth thee by the
way that thou shouldest go.*

Isaiah 48:17

Hear ... and receive my sayings; and the years of thy life shall be many. I have taught thee in the way of wisdom; I have led thee in right paths. When thou goest, thy steps shall not be straitened; and when thou runnest, thou shalt not stumble. Take fast hold of instruction; let her not go: keep her; for she is thy life.

Proverbs 4:10–13

Whoso keepeth the commandment shall feel no evil thing: and a wise man's heart discerneth both time and judgment.

Ecclesiastes 8:5

I know the thoughts that I think toward you, saith the LORD, thoughts of peace, and not of evil, to give you an expected end.

Jeremiah 29:11

The steps of a good man are ordered by the LORD: and he delighteth in his way.

Psalm 37:23

Godly Guidance
Reverend Jacqueline S. McClenney

In Judges 4, a military commander named Barak faced a difficult situation. He and his soldiers were being led into a confrontation with Sisera, an evil Gentile who had mightily oppressed the children of Israel for twenty years. Before the battle, Barak went to the prophetess Deborah and asked her for guidance.

Courageously, Deborah let Barak know that it was time to face Sisera. Led by God, she not only showed Barak the way, but she went with him as he faced the battle. Deborah could have received all of the fame and glory for the victory, but instead she gave all of the credit to the Lord. (Read her song in Judges 5.)

We have been given the leadership and guidance of the Holy Spirit to meet our daily challenges. Like Barak, let us look to those led by the Holy Spirit for guidance. And like Deborah, let us guide others with divine direction.

GOD'S WORDS OF LIFE ON
Health and Healing

Ye shall serve the LORD your God, and he shall bless thy bread, and thy water; and I will take sickness away from the midst of thee. There shall nothing cast their young, nor be barren, in thy land: the number of thy days I will fulfil.

Exodus 23:25–26

[The Messiah] was wounded for our transgressions, he was bruised for our iniquities: the chastisement of our peace was upon him; and with his stripes we are healed.

Isaiah 53:5

Because Christ also suffered for us, leaving us an example, that ye should follow his steps: ... Who his own self bare our sins in his own body on the tree, that we, being dead to sins, should live unto righteousness: by whose stripes ye were healed.

1 Peter 2:21, 24

"Unto you that fear my name shall the Sun of righteousness arise with healing in his wings," saith the LORD.

Malachi 4:2

GOD'S WORD OF LIFE ON
Health and Healing

Bless the LORD, O my soul, and forget not all his benefits: Who forgiveth all thine iniquities; who healeth all thy diseases.

Psalm 103:2–3

I will restore health unto thee, and I will heal thee of thy wounds, saith the LORD.

Jeremiah 30:17

Is any sick among you? let him call for the elders of the church; and let them pray over him, anointing him with oil in the name of the Lord: And the prayer of faith shall save the sick, and the Lord shall raise him up.

James 5:14–15

Heal me, O LORD, and I shall be healed; save me, and I shall be saved: for thou art my praise.

Jeremiah 17:14

I will extol thee, O LORD; for thou hast lifted me up, and hast not made my foes to rejoice over me. O LORD my God, I cried unto thee, and thou hast healed me.

Psalm 30:1–2

GOD'S WORDS OF LIFE ON
Health and Healing

*"If my people, which are called by my name,
shall humble themselves, and pray, and seek my
face, and turn from their wicked ways; then will I
hear from heaven, and will forgive their sin, and
will heal their land," saith the LORD.*

2 Chronicles 7:14

*Why art thou cast down, O my soul? and why art
thou disquieted within me? hope in God: for I
shall yet praise him, who is the health of my
countenance, and my God.*

Psalm 43:5

*Confess your faults one to another, and pray one
for another, that ye may be healed.*

James 5:16

*The LORD is nigh unto them that are of a broken
heart; and saveth such as be of a contrite spirit.*

Psalm 34:18

*"Behold, I will bring [my people] health and
cure, and I will cure them, and will reveal unto
them the abundance of peace and truth," saith the
LORD.*

Jeremiah 33:6

DEVOTIONAL THOUGHT ON
Health and Healing

Jesus: Our Hope for Wholeness
Bishop Frank Cummings

John describes a meeting between Jesus and a man who had been sick for 38 years. The man's last hope was to be the first person into a pool said to offer healing when the waters were stirred by an angel. After trying this fruitlessly for 38 years, the afflicted man was probably angry and profoundly discouraged.

Imagine his surprise when Jesus asked, "Wilt thou be made whole?" (John 5:6). What could the man say? His hope was so warped by years of unrelieved affliction that he probably wondered if he could face the disappointment of another failure. Then Jesus intervened. The man was healed and given entrance into a new life.

Jesus offered that man what even the angel could not—health, wholeness, the all-encompassing freedom from the prison of ill health. He offers it to us as well. Healing does not come only from angels, or physicians, or even medicine. Total healing ultimately comes from the God who gives new life. Jesus affirms, " I am life. Believe in me and you shall have life beyond the grip of pain and suffering."

Jesus said, "In my Father's house are many mansions: if it were not so, I would have told you. I go to prepare a place for you. And if I go and prepare a place for you, I will come again, and receive you unto myself; that where I am, there ye may be also."

John 14:2–3

Jesus said, "Verily I say unto you, Whatsoever ye shall bind on earth shall be bound in heaven: and whatsoever ye shall loose on earth shall be loosed in heaven."

Matthew 18:18

We know that if our earthly house of this tabernacle were dissolved, we have a building of God, an house not made with hands, eternal in the heavens.

2 Corinthians 5:1

Jesus said, "Behold, the kingdom of God is within you."

Luke 17:21

Blessed be the God and Father of our Lord Jesus Christ, which according to his abundant mercy hath begotten us again unto a lively hope by the resurrection of Jesus Christ from the dead, To an inheritance incorruptible, and undefiled, and that fadeth not away, reserved in heaven for you, Who are kept by the power of God through faith unto salvation ready to be revealed in the last time.

1 Peter 1:3–5

Jesus said, "Take no thought, saying, What shall we eat? or, What shall we drink? or, Where-withal shall we be clothed? ... for your heavenly Father knoweth that ye have need of all these things. But seek ye first the kingdom of God, and his righteousness; and all these things shall be added unto you.

Matthew 6:31–33

Wherefore we receiving a kingdom which cannot be moved, let us have grace, whereby we may serve God acceptably with reverence and godly fear.

Hebrews 12:28

*Thine, O LORD is the greatness, and the power,
and the glory, and the victory, and the majesty: for
all that is in the heaven and in the earth is thine;
thine is the kingdom, O LORD, and thou art exalted as head above all.*

I Chronicles 29:11

*Jesus said, "Rejoice not, that the spirits are subject
unto you; but rather rejoice, because your names
are written in heaven."*

Luke 10:20

*The Lord shall deliver me from every evil work,
and will preserve me unto his heavenly kingdom
to whom be glory for ever and ever.*

2 Timothy 4:18

*Hearken my beloved brethren, Hath not God
chosen the poor of this world rich in faith, and
heirs of the kingdom which he hath promised to
them that love him?*

James 2:5

This World Is Not Our Home

Dr. H. Michael Lemmons

Our entrance into this world happens without our consent. Likewise, the timing of our departure is fixed without our input. Indeed, the appointment with death is one we all must keep, and one for which we shall not be late. But we can take comfort in the fact that this earth, even with all that it has to offer, is not really our home.

We tend to become very accustomed to life on this planet. We instinctively fear or question death—the great unknown. But the truth of the matter is that we did not come here to stay.

What great consolation it is to know that the one in whom we believe—Jesus, the Lamb of God—has traveled this way before us. And not only that, he has prepared a place for us—a place that is truly our home, a place where we will spend eternity in his presence.

How can you be sure it's true? Jesus said so. And he not only spoke the truth; he *was* the Truth.

GOD'S WORDS OF LIFE ON
Honesty

Shew me thy ways, O LORD; teach me thy paths. Lead me in thy truth, and teach me: for thou art the God of my salvation; on thee do I wait all the day.

Psalm 25: 4–5

As for me, thou upholdest me in mine integrity, and settest me before thy face for ever, O LORD.

Psalm 41:12

Brethren, whatsoever things are true, whatsoever things are honest, whatsoever things are just, whatsoever things are pure, whatsoever things are lovely, whatsoever things are of good report; if there be any virtue, and if there be any praise, think on these things. Those things, which ye have both learned, and received, and heard, and seen in me, do: and the God of peace shall be with you.

Philippians 4:8–9

The LORD is nigh unto all them that call upon him, to all that call upon him in truth.

Psalm 145:18

*When much people were gathered together, and
were come to Jesus out of every city, he spake by a
parable: A sower went out to sow his seed: and as
he sowed, some fell by the way side; … And other
fell on good ground, and sprang up, and bare fruit
an hundredfold. … Now the parable is this: The
seed is the word of God. … That on the good
ground are they, which in an honest and good
heart, having heard the word, keep it, and bring
forth fruit with patience.*

Luke 8:4–5, 8, 11, 15

*Lying lips are abomination to the LORD: but they
that deal truly are his delight.*

Proverbs 12:22

*Judge me, O LORD; for I have walked in mine
integrity: I have trusted also in the LORD; therefore I shall not slide.*

Psalm 26:1

*I know … my God, that thou triest the heart, and
hast pleasure in uprightness.*

1 Chronicles 29:17

GOD'S WORDS OF LIFE ON
Honesty

The mouth of the just bringeth forth wisdom.

Proverbs 10:31

O keep my soul, and deliver me: let me not be ashamed; for I put my trust in thee. Let integrity and uprightness preserve me; for I wait on thee, O LORD.

Psalm 25:20–21

He that walketh uprightly walketh surely.

Proverbs 10:9

Behold, thou desirest truth in the inward parts, O God: and in the hidden part thou shalt make me to know wisdom.

Psalm 51:6

The LORD shall judge the people: judge me, O LORD, according to my righteousness, and according to mine integrity that is in me. Oh let the wickedness of the wicked come to an end; but establish the just: for the righteous God trieth the hearts and reins. My defence is of God, which saveth the upright in heart.

Psalm 7:8–10

Community Dishonesty
Reverend Dr. John Peoples, Ed.D.

The early church was a growing and thriving group of people deeply committed to each other and the meeting of each other's needs. All who had land or other possessions sold them and brought the proceeds and laid them at the apostles' feet. The money was distributed to those in need. Scripture also says that the believers "had all things common" (Acts 4:32).

Then we come to Acts 5, and a sour note is sounded. Pride entered the hearts of Ananias and Sapphira and caused them to lie about the sale of their property. Dishonesty and deceit had crept into the Christian community.

Dishonesty turns us into hypocrites— pretending to be something other than what we are. Our motives are not pure, and sin enters our hearts. When believers recognize the seriousness of sin and refuse to allow it to continue, the church of Jesus Christ will grow strong and see scores of unbelievers added to its number regularly.

The God of hope fill you with all joy and peace in believing, that ye may abound in hope, through the power of the Holy Ghost.

Romans 15:13

The LORD taketh pleasure in them that fear him, in those that hope in his mercy.

Psalm 147:11

Be of good courage, and God shall strengthen your heart, all ye that hope in the LORD.

Psalm 31:24

Whatsoever things were written aforetime were written for our learning, that we through patience and comfort of the scriptures might have hope.

Romans 15:4

Happy is he that hath the God of Jacob for his help, whose hope is in the LORD his God: Which made heaven, and earth, the sea, and all that therein is: which keepeth truth for ever.

Psalm 146:5–6

Being justified by faith, we have peace with God through our Lord Jesus Christ: By whom also we have access by faith into this grace wherein we stand, and rejoice in hope of the glory of God. And not only so, but we glory in tribulations also: knowing that tribulation worketh patience; And patience, experience; and experience, hope: and hope maketh not ashamed; because the love of God is shed abroad in our hearts by the Holy Ghost which is given unto us.

Romans 5:1–5

It is good that a man should both hope and quietly wait for the salvation of the LORD.

Lamentations 3:26

This I recall to my mind, therefore have I hope. It is of the LORD's mercies that we are not consumed, because his compassions fail not. They are new every morning: great is thy faithfulness. The LORD is my portion, saith my soul; therefore will I hope in him.

Lamentations 3:21–24

The grace of God that bringeth salvation hath appeared to all men, Teaching us that, denying ungodliness and worldly lusts, we should live soberly, righteously, and godly, in this present world; looking for that blessed hope, and the glorious appearing of the great God and our Saviour Jesus Christ.

Titus 2:11–13

Why art thou cast down, O my soul? and why art thou disquieted within me? hope in God: for I shall yet praise him, who is the health of my countenance, and my God.

Psalm 43:5

Who is a God like unto thee, that pardoneth iniquity, and passeth by the transgression of the remnant of his heritage? he retaineth not his anger for ever, because he delighteth in mercy. He will turn again, he will have compassion upon us; he will subdue our iniquities; and thou wilt cast all their sins into the depths of the sea.

Micah 7:18–19

Hope in God
Reverend Samuel Nixon, Jr.

Our desire for God will inevitably be less intense at times. At these moments we must say with the psalmist, "Hope thou in God: for I shall yet praise him for the help of his countenance" (Psalm 42:5).

Hope in God is essential to our being. Hope is a very present help in the time of trouble because God is the hope that is our help. He is our "refuge in times of trouble" (Psalm 9:9). He also assures us with the promise that, "Though I walk in the midst of trouble, thou wilt revive me" (Psalm 138:7).

Don't place your hope in the tangible . . . the mortal . . . the temporal things of life. Don't build your hopes on sands that slip away. Instead, build your hope on things eternal. Conclude as the psalmist did, "And now, Lord, what wait I for? my hope is in thee" (Psalm 39:7).

GOD'S WORDS OF LIFE ON
Humility

By humility and the fear of the LORD are riches,
and honour, and life.

Proverbs 22:4

The meek will God guide in judgment: and the
meek will he teach his way.

Psalm 25:9

Jesus called a little child unto him, and set him in
the midst of them, ... [and] said, "Whosoever
therefore shall humble himself as this little child,
the same is greatest in the kingdom of heaven."

Matthew 18:2, 4

Great is our LORD, and of great power: his
understanding is infinite. The LORD lifteth up
the meek.

Psalm 147:5–6

The fear of the LORD is the instruction of wis-
dom; and before honour is humility.

Proverbs 15:33

God resisteth the proud, but giveth grace unto the
humble. ... Humble yourselves in the sight of the
Lord, and he shall lift you up.

James 4:6, 10

God hath shewed strength with his arm; he hath scattered the proud in the imagination of their hearts. He hath put down the mighty from their seats, and exalted them of low degree. He hath filled the hungry with good things; and the rich he hath sent empty away.

Luke 1:51–53

The LORD taketh pleasure in his people: he will beautify the meek with salvation.

Psalm 149:4

All of you be subject one to another, and be clothed with humility: for God resisteth the proud, and giveth grace to the humble. Humble yourselves therefore under the mighty hand of God, that he may exalt you in due time: Casting all your care upon him; for he careth for you.

1 Peter 5:5–7

Jesus said, "Every one that exalteth himself shall be abased; and he that humbleth himself shall be exalted."

Luke 18:14

When pride cometh, then cometh shame: but with the lowly is wisdom.

Proverbs 11:2

GOD'S WORDS OF LIFE ON
Humility

Thus saith the high and lofty One that inhabiteth eternity, whose name is Holy; I dwell in the high and holy place, with him also that is of a contrite and humble spirit, to revive the spirit of the humble, and to revive the heart of the contrite ones.

Isaiah 57:15

Blessed are the poor in spirit; for their's is the kingdom of heaven. Blessed are the meek; for they shall inherit the earth.

Matthew 5:3, 5

He hath shewed thee, O man, what is good; and what doth the LORD require of thee, but to do justly, and to love mercy, and to walk humbly with thy God?

Micah 6:8

In thy majesty ride prosperously because of truth and meekness and righteous; and thy right hand shall teach thee.

Psalm 45:4

Boast in God
Reverend Ann Lightner-Fuller

To boast, vaunt, or brag means to express conceit about oneself or one's accomplishment. All three words suggest excessive pride, and all three are totally out of line with Christian character. The poorest person who understands and knows the Lord is wiser, mightier, and richer than all who trust in and boast in themselves.

In 1707, noted hymnologist Isaac Watts wrote these words: "When I survey the wondrous cross on which the Prince of Glory died, my richest gain I count, but whatever was to my profit I now consider loss for the sake of Christ, and pour contempt on all my pride." And in 1869, Frances Jane Van Alstyne penned in her famous hymn: "Jesus, keep me near the cross, be my glory ever, till my raptured soul shall find, rest beyond the river."

The cross reminds every Christian that we should boast in God who sent Jesus to atone for the sins of the world. The cross should keep us humble with hearts that are too full of thanksgiving to have room for boasting in our own accomplishments.

GOD'S WORDS OF LIFE ON
Joy

Jesus said, "Verily, verily, I say unto you, That ye shall weep and lament, but the world shall rejoice: and ye shall be sorrowful, but your sorrow shall be turned into joy. Ye now therefore have sorrow: but I will see you again, and your heart shall rejoice, and your joy no man taketh from you."

John 16:20, 22

They that sow in tears shall reap in joy. He that goeth forth and weepeth, bearing precious seed, shall doubtless come again with rejoicing, bringing his sheaves with him.

Psalm 126:5–6

Light is sown for the righteous, and gladness for the upright in heart.

Psalm 97:11

I will greatly rejoice in the LORD, my soul shall be joyful in my God; for he hath clothed me with the garments of salvation, he hath covered me with the robe of righteousness.

Isaiah 61:10

Blessed is every one that feareth the LORD; that walketh in his ways. For thou shalt eat the labour of thine hands: happy shalt thou be, and it shall be well with thee.

Psalm 128:1–2

Because the LORD thy God shall bless thee in all thine increase, and in all the works of thine hands, therefore thou shalt surely rejoice.

Deuteronomy 16:15

Jesus said, "Hitherto have ye asked nothing in my name: ask, and ye shall receive, that your joy may be full."

John 16:24

God giveth to a man that is good in his sight wisdom, and knowledge, and joy.

Ecclesiastes 2:26

Thou hast turned for me my mourning into dancing, O Lord: thou hast put off my sackcloth, and girded me with gladness.

Psalm 30:11

Thou wilt show me the path of life, O LORD: in thy presence is fulness of joy; at thy right hand there are pleasures for evermore.

Psalm 16:11

Thou, LORD, hast made me glad through thy work: I will triumph in the works of thy hands.

Psalm 92:4

Thou hast made known to me the ways of life; thou shalt make me full of joy with thy countenance, O God.

Acts 2:28

Happy is the man that finds wisdom, and the man that getteth understanding.

Proverbs 3:13

The ransomed of the LORD shall return, and come to Zion with songs and everlasting joy upon their heads: they shall obtain joy and gladness, and sorrow and sighing shall flee away.

Isaiah 35:10

*Behold, God is my salvation; I will trust, and not
be afraid: for the LORD JEHOVAH is my strength
and my song; he also is become my salvation.
Therefore with joy shall ye draw water out of the
wells of salvation. And in that day shall ye say,
Praise the LORD, call upon his name, declare his
doings among the people, make mention that his
name is exalted. Sing unto the LORD; for he hath
done excellent things: this is known in all the
earth. Cry out and shout, thou inhabitant of Zion:
for great is the Holy One of Israel in the midst
of thee.*

Isaiah 12:2–6

*Thou hast loved righteousness, and hated iniquity;
therefore God, even thy God, hath anointed thee
with the oil of gladness above thy fellows.*

Hebrews 1:9

*Now the God of hope fill you with all joy and
peace in believing, that ye may abound in hope,
through the power of the Holy Ghost.*

Romans 15:13

GOD'S WORDS OF LIFE ON
Joy

*O clap your hands, all ye people; shout unto God
with the voice of triumph. For the LORD ... is a
great King over all the earth.*

Psalm 47:1–2

*"Behold, I create new heavens and a new earth:
and the former shall not be remembered, nor
come into mind. Be ye glad and rejoice for ever in
that which I create: for, behold, I create Jerusalem
a rejoicing, and her people a joy. And I will
rejoice in Jerusalem, and joy in my people: and
the voice of weeping shall be no more heard in
her, nor the voice of crying," saith the LORD.*

Isaiah 65:17–19

*I have set the LORD always before me: because he
is at my right hand, I shall not be moved.
Therefore my heart is glad, and my glory
rejoiceth: my flesh also shall rest in hope.*

Psalm 16:8–9

Count It All Joy
Reverend Dr. J. Alfred Smith, Sr.

It seems strange to call suffering "a friend" when it gives us heartbreak and heartache. But the first chapter of James suggests that the purpose of suffering is to help, not to hurt. You and I are called to look past immediate hurt to see long-range good.

What is this long-range good? It is the maturation of our faith. The muscles of faith are strengthened through tribulation. Just as many physical athletes suffer from fatigue and burnout, many spiritual athletes run out of spiritual energy during times of suffering. Developing the spiritual disciplines of meditation, prayer, and Bible study helps mature our spiritual muscles.

In the midst of our increasing spiritual strength comes joy. There is joy in knowing that God has a loving purpose for our suffering and that no suffering lasts forever. There is joy in realizing that we do not bear our pain and suffering alone, for God is with us in our struggles. There is joy in knowing that trials cannot separate us from God's care but will bring us closer to him.

GOD'S WORDS OF LIFE ON
Kindness

Let him that glorieth glory in this, that he under-
standeth and knoweth me, that I am the LORD
which exercise lovingkindness, judgment, and
righteousness, in the earth: for in these things I
delight, saith the LORD.

Jeremiah 9:24

O praise the LORD, all ye nations: praise him, all
ye people. For his merciful kindness is great
toward us: and the truth of the LORD endureth
for ever. Praise ye the LORD.

Psalm 117:1–2

Who can find a virtuous woman: for her price is
far above rubies. ... She openeth her mouth with
wisdom; and in her tongue is the law of kindness.

Proverbs 31:10, 26

Let, I pray thee, O LORD, thy merciful kindness
be for my comfort, according to thy word unto
thy servant. Let thy tender mercies come unto me,
that I may live: for thy law is my delight.

Psalm 119:76–77

Blessed be the LORD: for he hath shown me his marvelous kindness in a strong city.

Psalm 31:21

And let us not be weary in well doing: for in due season we shall reap, if we faint not. As we have therefore opportunity, let us do good unto all men, especially unto them who are of the household of faith.

Galatians 6:9–10

The LORD hath made his wonderful works to be remembered: the LORD is gracious and full of compassion.

Psalm 111:4

We count them happy which endure. Ye have heard of the patience of Job, and have seen the end of the Lord; that the Lord is very pitiful, and of tender mercy.

James 5:11

Thou art a God ready to pardon, gracious and merciful, slow to anger, and of great kindness.

Nehemiah 9:17

GOD'S WORDS OF LIFE ON
Kindness

The mountains shall depart, and the hills be removed; but my kindness shall not depart from thee, neither shall the covenant of my peace be removed, saith the LORD that hath mercy on thee.

Isaiah 54:10

Unto the upright there ariseth light in the darkness: God is gracious, and full of compassion, and righteous.

Psalm 112:4

If ye turn again unto the LORD, your brethren and your children shall find compassion before them that lead them captive, so that they shall come again into this land: for the LORD your God is gracious and merciful, and will not turn away his face from you, if ye return unto him.

2 Chronicles 30:9

Thou, O LORD, art a God full of compassion, and gracious, longsuffering, and plenteous in mercy and truth.

Psalm 86:15

Kindness and Compassion

Reverend A. Charles Bowie

Jesus poured out his kindness and compassion on the multitudes as he ministered to their physical and spiritual needs. As God's messengers and members of the body of Christ, we must exhibit those same characteristics. The Scriptures instruct us, "If there be therefore any consolation in Christ, if any comfort of love, if any fellowship of the Spirit, if any bowels and mercies, fulfil ye my joy, that ye be likeminded, having the same love, being of one accord, of one mind" (Philippians 2:1–2).

When faced with families suffering the effects of crime, homelessness, illness, and loneliness, it's easy to become discouraged. But the Lord's kindness and compassion prevent us from losing hope. His encouragement enables us to encourage others who are struggling to survive.

We should also share with our children about the kindness and compassion of the Lord—teaching them that he will somehow make a way. And often that way is made when we allow God to use us as his instruments in the world.

GOD'S WORDS OF LIFE ON
Love

Jesus said, "He that hath my commandments, and keepeth them, he it is that loveth me: and he that loveth me shall be loved of my Father, and I will love him, and will manifest myself to him."

John 14:21

God who is rich in mercy, for his great love wherewith he loved us, Even when we were dead in sins hath quickened us together with Christ, (by grace ye are saved;) And hath raised us up together, and made us sit together in heavenly places in Christ Jesus.

Ephesians 2:4–6

If we love one another, God dwelleth in us, and his love is perfected in us.

1 John 4:12

Jesus said, "I say unto you, Love your enemies, bless them that curse you, do good to them that hate you, and pray for them which despitefully use you, and persecute you; That ye may be the children of your Father which is in heaven."

Matthew 5:44–45

Put on therefore, as the elect of God, holy and beloved, bowels of mercies, kindness, humbleness of mind, meekness, longsuffering. ... Above all these things put on charity, which is the bond of perfectness.

Colossians 3:12–14

Charity suffereth long, and is kind; charity envieth not; charity vaunteth not itself, is not puffed up, Doth not behave itself unseemly, seeketh not her own, is not easily provoked, thinketh no evil; Rejoiceth not in iniquity, but rejoiceth in the truth; Beareth all things, believeth all things, hopeth all things, endureth all things. Charity never faileth.

1 Corinthians 13:4–8

I am persuaded, that neither death, nor life, nor angels, nor principalities, nor powers, nor things present, nor things to come, nor height, nor depth, nor any other creature, shall be able to separate us from the love of God, which is in Christ Jesus our Lord.

Romans 8:38–39

GOD'S WORDS OF LIFE ON
Love

*Beloved, let us love one another: for love is of
God; and every one that loveth is born of God,
and knoweth God.*

1 John 4:7

*Jesus said, "If a man love me, he will keep my
words: and my Father will love him, and we will
come unto him, and make our abode with him."*

John 14:23

*There is no fear in love; but perfect love casteth
out fear.*

1 John 4:18

*The LORD hath appeared of old unto me, saying,
Yea, I have loved thee with an everlasting love:
therefore with lovingkindness have I drawn thee.*

Jeremiah 31:3

*The LORD openeth the eyes of the blind: the
LORD raiseth them that are bowed down: the
LORD loveth the righteous: The LORD preserveth
the strangers; he relieveth the fatherless and
widow.*

Psalm 146:8–9

The Real Thing
Reverend George R. LaSure

Love is our capacity to embrace others, despite their faults and inadequacies. It is the ability to "be there" for someone, no matter what. Real love is not only professed but acted upon and acted out. Love is putting all of our good intentions into action.

Jesus commands us to love one another in the same way that he has loved us: "As I have loved you, that ye also love one another. By this shall all men know that ye are my disciples, if ye have love one to another" (John 13:34–35).

As we love, we are to provide the care, nurturing, and support for our brothers and sisters that is essential to their well-being and their spiritual growth. Paul's famous love passage also says that love is something that grows stronger and ultimately becomes a physical and spiritual reality.

Love is immutable, genuine, and everlasting. Love is "The Real Thing!" God is Love!

GOD'S WORDS OF LIFE ON
Peace

Be careful for nothing; but in every thing by prayer and supplication with thanksgiving let your requests be made known unto God. The peace of God, which passeth all understanding, shall keep your hearts and minds through Christ Jesus.

Philippians 4:6–7

Now the Lord of peace himself give you peace always by all means. The Lord be with you all.

2 Thessalonians 3:16

Being justified by faith, we have peace with God through our Lord Jesus Christ: By whom also we have access by faith into this grace wherein we stand, and rejoice in hope of the glory of God.

Romans 5:1–2

Jesus said, "Peace I leave with you, my peace I give unto you: not as the world giveth, give I unto you. Let not your heart be troubled, neither let it be afraid."

John 14:27

God is not the author of confusion, but of peace.

1 Corinthians 14:33

Jesus said, "Blessed are the peacemakers: for they shall be called the children of God."

Matthew 5:9

Be perfect, be of good comfort, be of one mind, live in peace; and the God of love and peace shall be with you.

2 Corinthians 13:11

The wisdom that is from above is first pure, then peaceable, gentle, and easy to be intreated, full of mercy and good fruits, without partiality, and without hypocrisy. And the fruit of righteousness is sown in peace of them that make peace.

James 3:17–18

Glory, honour, and peace, to every man that worketh good, to the Jew first, and also to the Gentile; For there is no respect of persons with God.

Romans 2:10–11

When a man's ways please the LORD, he maketh even his enemies to be at peace with him.

Proverbs 16:7

GOD'S WORDS OF LIFE ON
Peace

For unto us a child is born, unto us a son is given:
and the government shall be upon his shoulder:
and his name shall be called Wonderful,
Counsellor, The mighty God, The everlasting
Father, The Prince of Peace.

Isaiah 9:6

The kingdom of God is not meat and drink; but
righteousness, and peace, and joy in the Holy
Ghost. For he that in these things serveth Christ is
acceptable to God, and approved of men. Let us
therefore follow after the things which make
for peace, and things wherewith one may
edify another.

Romans 14:17—19

Let the peace of God rule in your hearts, to the
which also ye are called in one body; and be ye
thankful.

Colossians 3:15

The God of hope fill you with all joy and peace
in believing, that ye may abound in hope,
through the power of the Holy Ghost.

Romans 15:13

Calling for Peace
Reverend Darryl I. Owens

In 2 Samuel 2, we read a story about the results of unnecessary competition among people of a common heritage. David had been established as the king of Judah. But Abner, the Secretary of Defense under the former administration placed Saul's son Ish-bosheth in office. This caused conflict between Israel and Judah. Men from both groups came together at Gibeon to take part in a contest, resulting in unnecessary bloodshed. Finally, someone spoke up for peace, and the battle was stopped.

This biblical story reminds us of life today. Unnecessary rivalries and disputes between friends and families result in shame, hurt feelings, retaliation, and even death. Violence and conflict perpetuate the cycles of grief and disruption of families.

Who will speak out for peace today? Where are the parents, children, siblings, grandparents, relatives, and friends who are willing to cry out to stop the fighting? When will we begin to value peace?

*The Lord direct your hearts into the love of God,
and into the patient waiting for Christ.*

2 Thessalonians 3:5

*The God of all grace, who hath called us unto his
eternal glory by Christ Jesus, after that ye have
suffered a while, make you perfect, stablish,
strengthen, settle you.*

1 Peter 5:10

*Blessed is the man that endureth temptation: for
when he is tried, he shall receive the crown of life,
which the Lord hath promised to them that
love him.*

James 1:12

*To them who by patient continuance in well
doing seek for glory and honour and immortality,
eternal life.*

Romans 2:7

*My brethren, count it all joy when ye fall into
divers temptations; Knowing this, that the trying
of your faith worketh patience.*

James 1:2–3

GOD'S WORD OF LIFE ON
Perseverance

This one thing I do, forgetting those things which are behind, and reaching forth unto those things which are before, I press toward the mark for the prize of the high calling of God in Christ Jesus.

Philippians 3:13–14

Our light affliction, which is but for a moment, worketh for us a far more exceeding and eternal weight of glory, While we look not at the things which are seen, but at the things which are not seen: for the things which are seen are temporal; but the things which are not seen are eternal.

2 Corinthians 4:17–18

Seeing we also are compassed about with so great a cloud of witnesses, let us lay aside every weight, and the sin which doth so easily beset us, and let us run with patience the race that is set before us, Looking unto Jesus the author and finisher of our faith.

Hebrews 12:1–2

GOD'S WORDS OF LIFE ON
Perseverance

Brethren, give diligence to make your calling and election sure: for if ye do these things, ye shall never fall: For so an entrance shall be ministered unto you abundantly into the everlasting kingdom of our Lord and Saviour Jesus Christ.

2 Peter 1:10–11

Blessed is the man that walketh not in the counsel of the ungodly, nor standeth in the way of sinners, nor sitteth in the seat of the scornful. But his delight is in the law of the LORD; and in his law doth he meditate day and night. And he shall be like a tree planted by the rivers of water, that bringeth forth his fruit in his season; his leaf also shall not wither; and whatsoever he doeth shall prosper.

Psalm 1:1–3

Whoso looketh into the perfect law of liberty, and continueth therein, he being not a forgetful hearer, but a doer of the work, this man shall be blessed in his deed.

James 1:25

DEVOTIONAL THOUGHT ON
Perseverance

Finish Your Course
Reverend Dr. Franklyn Richardson

When race kept Thurgood Marshall, the late Supreme Court Justice, from entering the University of Maryland law school, he chose to attend Howard. As a young attorney, he took *Brown v. the Board of Education* to the Supreme Court and won, legally dismantling "separate but equal" education for blacks and whites. During his years as a trial lawyer, he fought thirty-two significant civil rights cases.

As his body lay in state in the Supreme Court Building, long lines formed to say good-bye to a man who had not given up, dropped out, or failed to reach his goal. Justice Marshall kept his eye on the prize. He finished the course.

When you have fought the good fight, finished your course, and run the race set before you (2 Timothy 4:7), you won't have to wonder what it would have been like if you had given up and failed to reach your goal. You will have no regrets as you hear our Savior say, "Well done."

Praise the LORD with harp: sing unto him with the psaltery and an instrument of ten strings. Sing unto him a new song; play skillfully with a loud noise. For the word of the LORD is right; and all his works are done in truth.

Psalm 33:2–4

I will sing unto the LORD, for he hath triumphed gloriously. ... The LORD is my strength and song, and he is become my salvation: he is my God, and I will prepare him an habitation; my father's God, and I will exalt him.

Exodus 15:1–2

Thou art holy, O thou that inhabitest the praises of Israel. Our fathers trusted in thee: they trusted, and thou didst deliver them.

Psalm 22:3–4

Ye are a chosen generation, a royal priesthood, an holy nation, a peculiar people; that ye should show forth the praises of God who hath called you out of darkness into his marvellous light.

1 Peter 2:9

Let the saints be joyful in glory: let them sing aloud upon their beds. Let the high praises of God be in their mouth.

Psalm 149:5–6

Rejoice in the LORD, O ye righteous: for praise is comely for the upright.

Psalm 33:1

I will mention the lovingkindnesses of the LORD, and the praises of the LORD, according to all that the LORD hath bestowed on us, and the great goodness toward the house of Israel, which he hath bestowed on them according to his mercies, and according to the multitude of his lovingkindnesses. For he said, Surely they are my people, children that will not lie: so he was their Savior.

Isaiah 63:7–8

Praise ye the LORD. Sing unto the LORD a new song, and his praise in the congregation of saints. Let Israel rejoice in him that made him: let the children of Zion be joyful in their King.

Psalm 149:1–2

O come, let us worship and bow down: let us kneel before the LORD our maker. For he is our God; and we are the people of his pasture, and the sheep of his hand.

Psalm 95:6–7

Great is the LORD, and greatly to be praised: he also is to be feared above all gods.

1 Chronicles 16:25

A voice came out of the throne, saying, Praise our God, all ye his servants, and ye that fear him, both small and great. And I heard as it were the voice of a great multitude, and as the voice of many waters, and as the voice of mighty thunderings, saying, Alleluia: for the Lord God omnipotent reigneth.

Revelation 19:5–6

I will extol thee, O LORD; for thou hast lifted me up, and hast not made my foes to rejoice over me. O LORD my God, I cried unto thee, and thou hast healed me.

Psalm 30:1–2

Let them praise his name in the dance: let them sing praises unto him with the timbrel and harp. For the LORD taketh pleasure in his people: he will beautify the meek with salvation.

Psalm 149:3–4

I will praise thee, O LORD, with my whole heart; I will show forth all thy marvellous works. I will be glad and rejoice in thee: I will sing praise to thy name, O thou most High.

Psalm 9:1–2

Jesus saith, "The hour cometh, and now is, when the true worshippers shall worship the Father in spirit and in truth: for the Father seeketh such to worship him."

John 4:23

Give unto the LORD, O ye mighty, give unto the LORD glory and strength. Give unto the LORD the glory due unto his name; worship the LORD in the beauty of holiness.

Psalm 29:1–2

I will praise thee, Lord; for I am fearfully and wonderfully made: marvellous are thy works; and that my soul knoweth right well.

Psalm 139:14

The LORD is my strength and my shield; my heart trusted in him, and I am helped: therefore my heart greatly rejoiceth; and with my song will I praise him.

Psalm 28:7

O sing unto the LORD a new song; for he hath done marvelous things: his right hand, and his holy arm, hath gotten him the victory.

Psalm 98:1

I will sing unto the LORD as long as I live: I will sing praise to my God while I have my being. My meditation of him shall be sweet: I will be glad in the LORD.

Psalm 104:33–34

O praise the LORD, all ye nations: praise him, all ye people. For his merciful kindness is great toward us: and the truth of the LORD endureth for ever. Praise ye the LORD.

Psalm 117:1–2

DEVOTIONAL THOUGHT ON
Praise and Worship

Tender Hearts in Praise
Reverend Dr. Alan V. Ragland

When we open our hearts toward God in worship, we experience life-giving inspiration. In Psalm 95, the psalmist invites us: "O come, let us sing unto the LORD . . . Let us come before his presence with thanksgiving, and make a joyful noise unto him with psalms." You can sense the joyful enthusiasm with which this call is given.

Rather than being only spectators, we may actively participate in this glorious worship. First, the worship leader reminds us of the vastness of our Creator. When we behold his greatness, we become vessels for the praise of God.

Second, the psalmist instructs us about the intimacy of God, who has extended himself toward us in such a way that we can celebrate a shared identity. We are *God's* people and God is *our* God. In such a climate, the chilly fears of isolation and alienation dissipate in the warm breeze of the Spirit of God.

This is the confidence that we have in God, that, if we ask any thing according to his will, he heareth us: And if we know that he hear us, whatsoever we ask, we know that we have the petitions that we desired of him.

1 John 5:14–15

Jesus said, "Ask, and it shall be given you; seek, and ye shall find; knock, and it shall be opened unto you: For every one that asketh receiveth; and he that seeketh findeth; and to him that knocketh it shall be opened."

Matthew 7:7–8

"It shall come to pass, that before they call, I will answer; and while they are yet speaking, I will hear," saith the LORD.

Isaiah 65:24

Jesus said, "Whatsoever ye shall ask in my name, that will I do, that the Father may be glorified in the Son. If ye shall ask any thing in my name, I will do it."

John 14:13–14

GOD'S WORD OF LIFE ON
Prayer

Hearken unto the voice of my cry, my King, and my God: for unto thee will I pray. My voice shalt thou hear in the morning, O LORD; in the morning will I direct my prayer unto thee, and will look up.

Psalm 5:2–3

Jesus said, "Therefore I say unto you, What things soever ye desire, when ye pray, believe that ye receive them, and ye shall have them."

Mark 11:24

As for me, I shall call upon God; and the LORD shall save me. Evening, and morning, and at noon, will I pray, and cry aloud: and he shall hear my voice.

Psalm 55:16–17

Shall everyone that is godly pray unto thee, LORD, in a time when thou mayest be found: surely in the floods of great waters they shall not come nigh unto him.

Psalm 32:6

GOD'S WORDS OF LIFE ON
Prayer

The prayer of the upright is God's delight.

Proverbs 15:8

*"If my people, which are called by my name,
shall humble themselves, and pray, and seek my
face, and turn from their wicked ways; then will I
hear from heaven, and will forgive their sin, and
will heal their land," saith the Lord.*

2 Chronicles 7:14

*The prayer of faith shall save the sick, and the
Lord shall raise him up; and if he have committed
sins, they shall be forgiven him. Confess your
faults one to another, and pray one for another,
that ye may be healed.*

James 5:15–16

*The eyes of the Lord are over the righteous, and
his ears are open unto their prayers.*

1 Peter 3:12

*Jesus said, "All things, whatsoever ye shall ask in
prayer, believing, ye shall receive."*

Matthew 21:21–22

GOD'S WORD OF LIFE ON
Prayer

Jesus said, "Whatsoever ye shall ask the Father in my name, he will give it you."

John 16:23

The Lord has heard the voice of my weeping. The LORD hath heard my supplication; the LORD will receive my prayer.

Psalm 6:8–9

The Spirit ... helpeth our infirmities: for we know not what we should pray for as we ought: but the Spirit itself maketh intercession for us with groanings which cannot be uttered. And he that searcheth the hearts knoweth what is the mind of the Spirit, because he maketh intercession for the saints according to the will of God.

Romans 8:26–27

"Because he hath set his love upon me, therefore will I deliver him: I will set him on high, because he hath known my name. He shall call upon me, and I will answer him: I will be with him in trouble; I will deliver him, and honour him," saith the LORD.

Psalm 91:14–15

Continue in prayer, and watch in the same with thanksgiving.

Colossians 4:2

Jesus is able also to save them to the uttermost that come unto God by him, seeing he ever liveth to make intercession for them.

Hebrews 7:25

Who shall lay any thing to the charge of God's elect? It is God that justifieth. Who is he that condemneth? It is Christ that died, yea rather, that is risen again, who is even at the right hand of God, who also maketh intercession for us.

Romans 8:33–34

God will regard the prayer of the destitute, and not despise their prayer.

Psalm 102:17

Jesus said, "When ye stand praying, forgive, if ye have ought against any: that your Father also which is in heaven may forgive you your trespasses. But if ye do not forgive, neither will your Father in heaven forgive your trespasses."

Mark 11:25–26

"If My People . . ."
Reverend Joseph A. Darby

We live in a technologically advanced, complex, and competitive world. Many of us lose time, health, and peace trying to keep up with life's race; sometimes we succumb to the stress of trying and fail to find reasonable solutions to difficult problems. We would do well in such times to return to our ancestors' practice of prayer.

Having endured the horrors of slavery and brutal racism, they had a simple faith that proclaimed, "Up above my head, I see glory in the air, there must be a God somewhere."

Take time each day to pause in the midst of life's pressures to look to the Lord. Look prayerfully, humbly, and obediently to Christ, who brings prosperity and peace when the storms of life are raging. When we do so as individuals and as a Christian community, then we can cut through life's complexities and find peace and direction that the world cannot offer.

GOD'S WORDS OF LIFE ON
Protection

Fear thou not; for I am with thee: be not dismayed; for I am thy God: I will strengthen thee; yea, I will help thee; yea, I will uphold thee with the right hand of my righteousness.

Isaiah 41:10

In the time of trouble God shall hide me in his pavilion: in the secret of his tabernacle shall he hide me; he shall set me up upon a rock.

Psalm 27:5

The beloved of the LORD shall dwell in safety by him; and the LORD shall cover him all the day long, and he shall dwell between his shoulders.

Deuteronomy 33:12

Thou shalt not be afraid for the terror by night; nor for the arrow that flieth by day; Nor for the pestilence that walketh in darkness; nor for the destruction that wasteth at noonday. A thousand shall fall at thy side, and ten thousand at thy right hand; but it shall not come nigh thee.

Psalm 91:5–7

We may boldly say, The Lord is my helper, and I will not fear what man shall do unto me.

Hebrews 13:6

God layeth up sound wisdom for the righteous: he is a buckler to them that walk uprightly. He keepeth the paths of judgment, and preserveth the way of his saints.

Proverbs 2:7–8

The Lord shall deliver me from every evil work, and will preserve me unto his heavenly kingdom: to whom be glory for ever and ever.

2 Timothy 4:18

Cast thy burden upon the LORD, and he shall sustain thee: he shall never suffer the righteous to be moved.

Psalm 55:22

In the fear of the LORD is strong confidence: and his children shall have a place of refuge.

Proverbs 14:26

GOD'S WORDS OF LIFE ON
Protection

The LORD is thy keeper: the LORD is thy shade upon thy right hand. The sun shall not smite thee by day, nor the moon by night. The LORD shall preserve thee from all evil: he shall preserve thy soul. The LORD shall preserve thy going out and thy coming in from this time forth, and even for evermore.

Psalm 121:5–8

The eternal God is thy refuge, and underneath are the everlasting arms.

Deuteronomy 33:27

The LORD loveth judgment, and forsaketh not his saints; they are preserved for ever.

Psalm 37:28

The name of the LORD is a strong tower: the righteous runneth into it, and is safe.

Proverbs 18:10

I will be glad and rejoice in thy mercy, LORD: for thou hast considered my trouble; thou hast known my soul in adversities; And hast not shut me up into the hand of the enemy: thou hast set my feet in a large room.

Psalm 31:7–8

I will say of the LORD, He is my refuge and my fortress: my God; in him will I trust. Surely he shall deliver thee from the snare of the fowler, and from the noisome pestilence. He shall cover thee with his feathers, and under his wings shalt thou trust: his truth shall be thy shield and buckler.

Psalm 91:2–4

Every word of God is pure: he is a shield unto them that put their trust in him.

Proverbs 30:5

I am persuaded, that neither death, nor life, nor angels, nor principalities, nor powers, nor things present, nor things to come, Nor height, nor depth, nor any other creature, shall be able to separate us from the love of God, which is in Christ Jesus our Lord.

Romans 8:38–39

Keep me as the apple of the eye, hide me under the shadow of thy wings, O LORD.

Psalm 17:8

GOD'S WORDS OF LIFE ON
Protection

In thee, O LORD, do I put my trust: let me never be put to confusion. Deliver me in thy righteousness, and cause me to escape: incline thine ear unto me, and save me. Be thou my strong habitation, whereunto I may continually resort: thou hast given commandment to save me; for thou art my rock and my fortress.

Psalm 71:1–3

The fear of man bringeth a snare: but whoso putteth his trust in the LORD shall be safe.

Proverbs 29:25

The angel of the LORD encampeth round about them that fear him, and delivereth them.

Psalm 34:7

The salvation of the righteous is of the LORD: he is their strength in the time of trouble. The LORD shall help them, and deliver them: he shall deliver them from the wicked, and save them, because they trust in him.

Psalm 37:39–40

DEVOTIONAL THOUGHT ON
Protection

Help in the Time of Trouble
Reverend Dr. H. Devore Chapman

In spite of life's troubles, Psalm 46 affirms the believer's solid declaration: "we will not fear." What a powerful position! The psalmist reveals to the world that we have no fear because "God is our refuge and strength." Our God offers us a place of protection. We remain in his protective care and he promises his presence in the time of trouble.

According to the psalmist, God also brings about his purposes. The psalmist invites us to witness all that God has done: "Come, behold the works of the LORD … He maketh wars to cease unto the end of the earth; he breaketh the bow, and cutteth the spear in sunder; he burneth the chariot in the fire." Further, we are instructed to "Be still, and know that I am God." He alone is sovereign.

No matter what your troubles may be, remember your position and God's protection. Thanks be to God that he will help us in the time of trouble!

*Now therefore fear ye not: I will nourish you,
and your little ones. And he comforted them, and
spake kindly unto them.*

Genesis 50:21

*God is able to make all grace abound toward you;
that ye, always having all sufficiency in all things,
may abound to every good work. ... God that
ministereth seed to the sower both minister bread
for your food, and multiply your seed sown, and
increase the fruits of your righteousness; Being
enriched in every thing to all bountifulness, which
causeth through us thanksgiving to God.*

2 Corinthians 9:8, 10–11

*Jesus said, "Wherefore, if God so clothe the grass
of the field, which to day is, and to morrow is cast
into the oven, shall he not much more clothe you,
O ye of little faith? Therefore take no thought,
saying, What shall we eat? or, What shall we
drink? or, Wherewithal shall we be clothed? ...
for your heavenly Father knoweth that ye have
need of all these things."*

Matthew 6:30–32

GOD'S WORD OF LIFE ON
Provision

Jesus said, "What man is there of you, whom if his son ask bread, will he give him a stone? Or if he ask a fish, will he give him a serpent? If ye then, being evil, know how to give good gifts unto your children, how much more shall your Father which is in heaven give good things to them that ask him?"

Matthew 7:9–11

The LORD shall guide thee continually, and satisfy thy soul in drought, and make fat thy bones: and thou shalt be like a watered garden, and like a spring of water, whose waters fail not.

Isaiah 58:11

God left not himself without witness, in that he did good, and gave us rain from heaven, and fruitful seasons, filling our hearts with food and gladness.

Acts 14:17

"My people shall be satisfied with my goodness," saith the LORD.

Jeremiah 31:14

God's Words of Life on
Provision

I have been young, and now am old; yet have I not seen the righteous forsaken, nor his seed begging bread. He is ever merciful, and lendeth; and his seed is blessed.

Psalm 37:25–26

My God shall supply all your need according to his riches in glory by Christ Jesus.

Philippians 4:19

Jesus said, "Consider the ravens: for they neither sow nor reap; which neither have storehouse nor barn; and God feedeth them: how much more are ye better than the fowls? ... Seek not ye what ye shall eat, or what ye shall drink, neither be ye of doubtful mind. For all these things do the nations of the world seek after: and your Father knoweth that ye have need of these things. But rather seek ye the kingdom of God; and all these things shall be added unto you."

Luke 12:24, 29–31

All Things Are Possible

Reverend Rodney Sadler

Being a single parent is difficult in any age. In 2 Kings 4, we read the story of a widow who appealed for help to Elisha, the servant of God. She told him that her husband's creditors were threatening to take her two sons as slaves. This widow believed that her God would liberate her and ensure the safety of her family.

If you are a single parent struggling to maintain the health and safety of your family, remember that you have an ally on high. He may give you ideas for making the budget stretch or provide employment. He may provide support in the form of a caring church community. He may provide just the right person at just the right time—in the same way he provided Elisha to help the widow.

For a single parent, keeping a family together may never be easy, but take heart. With God on your side, "all things are possible" (Matthew 19:26).

GOD'S WORDS OF LIFE ON
Relationships

Jesus said, "If ye abide in me, and my words abide in you, ye shall ask what ye will, and it shall be done unto you."

John 15:7

Jesus said, "Behold, I stand at the door, and knock: if any man hear my voice, and open the door, I will come in to him, and will sup with him, and he with me."

Revelation 3:20

A man that hath friends must show himself friendly: and there is a friend that sticketh closer than a brother.

Proverbs 18:24

Jesus said, "Greater love hath no man than this, that a man lay down his life for his friends. Ye are my friends, if ye do whatsoever I command you. Henceforth I call you not servants; for the servant knoweth not what his lord doeth: but I have called you friends; for all things that I have heard of my Father I have made known unto you."

John 15:13–15

*A friend loveth at all times, and a brother is born
for adversity.*

Proverbs 17:17

*Two are better than one; because they have a
good reward for their labour. For if they fall, the
one will lift up his fellow: but woe to him that is
alone when he falleth; for he hath not another to
help him up. Again, if two lie together, then they
have heat: but how can one be warm alone? And
if one prevail against him, two shall withstand
him; and a threefold cord is not quickly broken.*

Ecclesiastes 4:9–12

*Faithful are the wounds of a friend; but the kisses
of an enemy are deceitful.*

Proverbs 27:6

*I will receive you, and will be a Father unto you,
And ye shall be my sons and daughters, saith the
Lord Almighty.*

2 Corinthians 6:17–18

*Iron sharpeneth iron; so a man sharpeneth the
countenance of his friend.*

Proverbs 27:17

GOD'S WORDS OF LIFE ON
Relationships

When my father and my mother forsake me, then the LORD will take me up.

Psalm 27:10

Jesus spake, saying, "Lo, I am with you always, even unto the end of the world."

Matthew 28:20

The LORD saith, "I will betroth thee unto me for ever; yea, I will betroth thee unto me in right-eousness, and in judgment, and in lovingkindness, and in mercies. I will even betroth thee unto me in faithfulness: and thou shalt know the LORD."

Hosea 2:19–20

He that walketh with wise men shall be wise.

Proverbs 13:20

If we walk in the light, as he is in the light, we have fellowship one with another, and the blood of Jesus Christ his Son cleanseth us from all sin.

1 John 1:7

The Blessing of Divine Kinship

Dr. Clarence G. Newsome

Human relationships are established in a variety of ways, as we see in the story of Abraham, Sarah, Hagar, Ishmael and Isaac. Abraham and Sarah are related by marriage; Abraham and Hagar are related by concubinage; Abraham and Ishmael are related by blood; so too are Hagar and Ishmael, and Sarah and Isaac. By means of the unenviable estate of bondage, Hagar and Ishmael are related to Sarah.

The family story related in Genesis 16 shows us that our effort to rely wholly on the perceived advantages of blood relationships to develop families, communities and nations can prove disastrous if we lose sight of the ground of all human relationships—our kinship to God. Families, communities and nations are rooted in divine kinship. The birth of Isaac as well as the liberation and survival of Hagar and Ishmael result from God's kinship.

Our kinship with God is a wonderful blessing. It frees all God's children to live together.

Jesus said, "Likewise, I say unto you, there is joy in the presence of the angels of God over one sinner that repenteth.

Luke 15:10

Repent, and be baptized every one of you in the name of Jesus Christ for the remission of sins, and ye shall receive the gift of the Holy Ghost.

Acts 2:38

Jesus said, "I say unto you, that likewise joy shall be in heaven over one sinner that repenteth, more than over ninety and nine just persons, which need no repentance."

Luke 15:7

The Lord is not slack concerning his promise, as some men count slackness; but is longsuffering to us-ward, not willing that any should perish, but that all should come to repentance.

2 Peter 3:9

Thou, LORD, art good, and ready to forgive; and plenteous in mercy unto all them that call upon thee.

Psalm 86:5

GOD'S WORD OF LIFE ON
Repentance

Jesus said, "They that are whole need not a physician; but they that are sick. I came not to call the righteous, but sinners to repentance."

Luke 5:31–32

Let the wicked forsake his way, and the unrighteous man his thoughts: and let him return unto the LORD, and he will have mercy upon him; and to our God, for he will abundantly pardon.

Isaiah 55:7

"If the wicked will turn from all his sins that he hath committed, and keep all my statutes, and do that which is lawful and right, he shall surely live, he shall not die," saith the LORD.

Ezekiel 18:21

Thus saith the Lord GOD, the Holy One of Israel; In returning and rest shall ye be saved; in quietness and in confidence shall be your strength.

Isaiah 30:15

If we confess our sins, God is faithful and just to forgive us our sins, and to cleanse us from all unrighteousness.

1 John 1:9

GOD'S WORDS OF LIFE ON
Repentance

First God, having raised up his Son Jesus, sent him to bless you, in turning away everyone of you from his iniquities.

Acts 3:26

The LORD is nigh unto them that are of a broken heart; and saveth such as be of a contrite spirit.

Psalm 34:18

Repent ye therefore, and be converted, that your sins may be blotted out, when the times of refreshing shall come from the presence of the Lord. He shall send Jesus Christ, which before was preached unto you: Whom the heaven must receive until the times of restitution of all things, which God hath spoken by the mouth of all his holy prophets since the world began.

Acts 3:19–21

If my people, which are called by my name, shall humble themselves, and pray, and seek my face, and turn from their wicked ways; then will I hear from heaven, and will forgive their sin, and will heal their land.

2 Chronicles 7:14

A New Heart

Reverend Benjamin W. Noble

Our nation is sick. It has a bad heart. Our nation and its people need a major operation: a heart transplant.

Ezekiel reminds us that we don't have to suffer with the symptoms of a bad heart. Repentance is the operation we need, and God promises that if we repent, he will give us a new heart: "A new heart also will I give you, and a new spirit will I put within you: and I will take away the stony heart out of your flesh, and I will give you an heart of flesh. And I will put my spirit within you, and cause you to walk in my statues, and ye shall keep my judgments, and do them" (Ezekiel 36:26–27).

Repentance before the Lord results in receiving a new heart and the life-giving spirit. The new heart produces love, joy, peace, kindness, goodness, fidelity, gentleness, and self-control. God's promised restoration and preservation are the reward. Hear! See! God is for us!

*Jesus said, "Verily I say unto you, There is no
man that hath left house, or brethren, or sisters, or
father, or mother, or wife, or children, or lands,
for my sake, and the gospel's, But he shall receive
an hundredfold now in this time, houses, and
brethren, and sisters, and mothers, and children,
and lands, with persecutions; and in the world to
come eternal life."*

Mark 10:29–31

*Whatsoever good thing any man doeth, the same
shall he receive of the Lord.*

Ephesians 6:8

*Jesus said, "Whosoever shall give to drink unto
one of these little ones a cup of cold water only in
the name of a disciple, verily I say unto you, he
shall in no wise lose his reward."*

Matthew 10:42

*I the LORD search the heart, I try the reins, even
to give every man according to his ways, and
according to the fruit of his doings.*

Jeremiah 17:10

According to the grace of God which is given unto me, as a wise masterbuilder, I have laid the foundation, and another buildeth theron. But let every man take heed how he buildeth thereupon. For other foundation can no man lay than that is laid, which is Jesus Christ. Now if any man build upon this foundation gold, silver, precious stones, wood, hay, stubble; Every man's work shall be made manifest: for the day shall declare it, because it shall be revealed by fire; and the fire shall try every man's work of what sort it is. If any man's work abide which he hath built thereupon, he shall receive a reward.

1 Corinthians 3:10–14

Look to yourselves, that we lose not those things which we have wrought, but that we receive a full reward. ... He that abideth in the doctrine of Christ, he hath both the Father and the Son.

2 John 1:8–9

He that followeth after righteousness and mercy findeth life, righteousness, and honour.

Proverbs 21:21

Jesus said, "Fear not, little flock; for it is your Father's good pleasure to give you the kingdom."

Luke 12:32

Jesus said, "Verily I say unto you, There is no man that hath left house, or parents, or brethren, or wife, or children, for the kingdom of God's sake, Who shall not receive manifold more in this present time, and in the world to come life everlasting."

Luke 18:29–30

O love the LORD, all ye his saints: for the LORD preserveth the faithful, and plentifully rewardeth the proud doer.

Psalm 31:23

Jesus said, "Love ye your enemies, and do good, and lend, hoping for nothing again; and your reward shall be great, and ye shall be the children of the Highest."

Luke 6:35

Reward

Does It Pay?
Bishop Ithiel C. Clemmons

King Hezekiah was facing a terminal illness and certain death. He prayed, "'O LORD, remember how I have walked before thee in truth and with a perfect heart, and have done that which is good in thy sight.' And Hezekiah wept sore" (2 Kings 20:3). The Lord graciously responded, "I have heard thy prayer, I have seen thy tears: behold, I will heal thee" (2 Kings 20:5).

The story of Hezekiah demonstrates a pattern: righteousness, prayer, grace, healing, deliverance. This story became a favorite for our enslaved forebears. They took the narrative as their own for it bore an unmistakable witness to one claim that God is powerfully although unpredictably present in situations of oppression, exploitation, personal need, sickness, and death.

If your ultimate concern is fame, fortune, or human affirmation, serving God does *not* pay. However, if your desire is to please God, to be salt in the earth, and a light in the world, it *does* pay. Faithful living *does* have a reward!

GOD'S WORDS OF LIFE ON
Righteousness

Thou openest thine hand, and satisfiest the desire of every living thing. The LORD is righteous in all his ways, and holy in all his works. The LORD is nigh unto all them that call upon him, to all that call upon him in truth. He will fulfil the desire of them that fear him: he also will hear their cry, and will save them.

Psalm 145:16–19

Jesus said, "Blessed are they which do hunger and thirst after righteousness: for they shall be filled." "Blessed are they which are persecuted for right- eousness' sake: for theirs is the kingdom of heaven."

Matthew 5:6, 10

The fear of the wicked, it shall come upon him: but the desire of the righteous shall be granted. As the whirlwind passeth, so is the wicked no more: but the righteous is an everlasting foundation.

Proverbs 10:24–25

The work of righteousness shall be peace; and the effect of righteousness quietness and assurance for ever.

Isaiah 32:17

Better is a little with righteousness than great revenues without right.

Proverbs 16:8

A good man showeth favour, and lendeth: he will guide his affairs with discretion. Surely he shall not be moved for ever: the righteous shall be in everlasting remembrance.

Psalm 112:5–6

Blessed is the man that feareth the LORD, that delighteth greatly in his commandments. His seed shall be mighty upon earth: the generation of the upright shall be blessed. Wealth and riches shall be in his house: and his righteousness endureth for ever.

Psalm 112:1–3

If any man sin, we have an advocate with the Father, Jesus Christ the righteous: And he is the propitiation for our sins: and not for ours only, but also for the sins of the whole world.

1 John 2:1–2

GOD'S WORDS OF LIFE ON
R i g h t e o u s n e s s

He that followeth after righteousness and mercy findeth life, righteousness, and honour.

Proverbs 21:21

The LORD will not cast off his people, neither will he forsake his inheritance. But judgment shall return unto righteousness: and all the upright in heart shall follow it.

Psalm 94:14–15

The wicked flee when no man pursueth: but the righteous are bold as a lion.

Proverbs 28:1

The LORD God is a sun and shield: the LORD will give grace and glory: no good thing will he withhold from them that walk uprightly.

Psalm 84:11

Now the righteousness of God without the law is manifested, being witnessed by the law and the prophets; even the righteousness of God which is by faith of Jesus Christ unto all and upon all them that believe.

Romans 3:21–22

Righteousness Through Faith

Reverend Samuel Nixon, Jr.

Ultimately everyone should ask: "Am I living a righteous life?" Paul answered this question with the words of the psalmist: "There is none righteous, no, not one" (Romans 3:10).

Righteousness does not come to us naturally. Neither does it come by chance. It is not an "oops" type of thing! No, righteousness must come from the source of all righteousness—God! And faith in Jesus Christ is the key to claiming righteousness, for we are "justified freely by his grace through the redemption that is in Christ Jesus ... Therefore we conclude that a man is justified by faith without the deeds of the law" (Romans 3:24, 28).

This justification by faith is good for everyone. Like an insurance policy, it provides a comprehensive plan of coverage, *leaving no one out* who wants to be in! If we want to declare our righteousness to the world, we've got to do it through faith in God through Christ Jesus. There is no other way!

GOD'S WORDS OF LIFE ON
Salvation

"Because he hath set his love upon me, therefore will I deliver him: I will set him on high, because he hath known my name. He shall call upon me, and I will answer him: I will be with him in trouble; I will deliver him, and honour him. With long life will I satisfy him, and show him my salvation," saith the LORD.

Psalm 91:14–16

There is one God, and one mediator between God and men, the man Christ Jesus; Who gave himself a ransom for all, to be testified in due time.

1 Timothy 2:5–6

If thou shalt confess with thy mouth the Lord Jesus, and shalt believe in thine heart that God hath raised him from the dead, thou shalt be saved. For with the heart man believeth unto righteousness; and with the mouth confession is made unto salvation.

Romans 10:9–10

The angel of the LORD encampeth round about them that fear him, and delivereth them.

Psalm 34:7

GOD'S WORD OF LIFE ON
Salvation

*God saith, I have heard thee in a time accepted,
and in the day of salvation have I succoured thee:
behold, now is the accepted time; behold, now is
the day of salvation.*

2 Corinthians 6:2

*To Christ give all the prophets witness, that
through his name whosoever believeth in him
shall receive remission of sins.*

Acts 10:43

*Jesus said, "He that believeth and is baptized shall
be saved."*

Mark 16:16–18

*Being made perfect, Christ became the author of
eternal salvation unto all them that obey him.*

Hebrews 5:9

*For God so loved the world, that he gave his only
begotten Son, that whosoever believeth in him
should not perish, but have everlasting life. God
sent not his Son into the world to condemn the
world; but that the world through him might be
saved.*

John 3:16–17

GOD'S WORDS OF LIFE ON
Salvation

Jesus said, "I am the door: by me if any man enter in, he shall be saved, and shall go in and out, and find pasture."

John 10:9

Fear ye not, stand still, and see the salvation of the LORD, which he will show to you today.

Exodus 14:13

Look unto me, and be ye saved, all the ends of the earth: for I am God, and there is none else.

Isaiah 45:22

Salvation belongeth unto the LORD: thy blessing is upon thy people.

Psalm 3:8

The LORD is my strength and song, and he is become my salvation: he is my God, and I will prepare him an habitation; my father's God, and I will exalt him.

Exodus 15:2

All have sinned, and come short of the glory of God; Being justified freely by his grace through the redemption that is in Christ Jesus: Whom God hath set forth to be a propitiation through faith in his blood, to declare his righteousness for the remission of sins that are past, through the forbearance of God; To declare, I say, at this time his righteousness: that he might be just, and the justifier of him which believeth in Jesus.

Romans 3:23–26

Christ was once offered to bear the sins of many; and unto them that look for him shall he appear the second time without sin unto salvation.

Hebrews 9:28

God commendeth his love toward us, in that, while we were yet sinners, Christ died for us. Much more then, being now justified by his blood, we shall be saved from wrath through him.

Romans 5:8–9

Herein is love, not that we loved God, but that he loved us, and sent his son to be the propitiation for our sins.

1 John 4:10

As they were eating, Jesus took bread, and blessed it, and brake it, and gave it to the disciples, and said, Take, eat; this is my body. And he took the cup, and gave thanks, and gave it to them, saying, Drink ye all of it; This is my blood of the new testament, which is shed for many for the remission of sins.

Matthew 26:26–28

In Christ Jesus ye who sometimes were far off are made nigh by the blood of Christ. For he is our peace, who hath made both one, and hath broken down the middle wall of partition between us.

Ephesians 2:13–14

Behold, the eye of the LORD is upon them that fear him, upon them that hope in his mercy; To deliver their soul from death, and to keep them alive in famine.

Psalm 33:18–19

*God hath made Christ to be sin for us, who knew
no sin; that we might be made the righteousness
of God in him.*

2 Corinthians 5:21

*Hereunto were ye called: because Christ also suf-
fered for us, leaving us an example, that ye should
follow his steps. ... Who his own self bare our sins
in his own body on the tree, that we, being dead
to sins, should live unto righteousness: by whose
stripes ye were healed. For ye were as sheep going
astray; but are now returned unto the Shepherd
and Bishop of your souls.*

1 Peter 2:21, 24–25

*If the blood of bulls and of goats, and the ashes of
an heifer sprinkling the unclean, sanctifieth to the
purifying of the flesh: how much more shall the
blood of Christ, who through the eternal Spirit
offered himself without spot to God, purge your
conscience from dead works to serve the living
God?*

Hebrews 9:13–14

GOD'S WORDS OF LIFE ON
Salvation

Ye know that ye were not redeemed with corruptible things, as silver and gold, from your vain conversation received by tradition from your fathers; But with the precious blood of Christ, as of a lamb without blemish and without spot.

1 Peter 1:18–19

The salvation of the righteous is of the LORD: he is their strength in the time of trouble.

Psalm 37:39

You, being dead in your sins and the uncircumcision of your flesh, hath he quickened together with him, having forgiven you all trespasses; Blotting out the handwriting of ordinances that was against us, which was contrary to us, and took it out of the way, nailing it to his cross.

Colossians 2:13–14

Truly my soul waiteth upon God: from him cometh my salvation. He only is my rock and my salvation; he is my defence; I shall not be greatly moved.

Psalm 62:1–2

All Who Call on Him
Reverend Dr. Arthur L. Wilson

In Romans 9, salvation is defined as a work of God's sovereign choice. God chooses the method of salvation and the means by which it is offered, as well as the recipients of his salvation.

Salvation is not tied to any human agency, race, class, gender or social standing. All have sinned; God's grace is offered equally to everyone. Those who desire salvation must come humbly confessing their sins, accepting the lordship of Jesus Christ and committing themselves to live according to God's Word. Salvation is simple, yet profound. God so loved us that he sent Jesus Christ to die to redeem our souls and to rise triumphant over Satan, that we might live triumphant over Satan.

God's faithful church must teach these essential truths and nurture Christian maturity in all believers. As we are faithful to our mission and ministry, God will cause the church to grow spiritually and numerically.

GOD'S WORDS OF LIFE ON
Self-Esteem

"Can a woman forget her sucking child, that she should not have compassion on the son of her womb? yea, they may forget, yet will I not forget thee. Behold, I have graven thee upon the palms of my hands; thy walls are continually before me," saith the LORD.

Isaiah 49:15–16

We are God's workmanship, created in Christ Jesus unto good works, which God hath before ordained that we should walk in them.

Ephesians 2:10

Cast not away ... your confidence, which hath great recompence of reward. For ye have need of patience, that, after ye have done the will of God, ye might receive the promise.

Hebrews 10:35

Jesus said, "Are not two sparrows sold for a farthing? and one of them shall not fall on the ground without your Father. But the very hairs of your head are all numbered. Fear ye not therefore, ye are of more value than many sparrows."

Matthew 10:29–31

GOD'S WORD OF LIFE ON
Self-Esteem

Know ye that the LORD he is God: it is he that hath made us, and not we ourselves; we are his people, and the sheep of his pasture.

Psalm 100:3

Blessed be the God and Father of our Lord Jesus Christ, who hath blessed us with all spiritual blessings in heavenly places in Christ: According as he hath chosen us in him before the foundation of the world, that we should be holy and without blame before him in love: Having predestinated us unto the adoption of children by Jesus Christ to himself, according to the good pleasure of his will, To the praise of the glory of his grace, wherein he hath made us accepted in the beloved.

Ephesians 1:3–6

The LORD hath appeared of old unto me, saying, Yea, I have loved thee with an everlasting love: therefore with lovingkindness have I drawn thee.

Jeremiah 31:3

Jesus said, "My grace is sufficient for thee: for my strength is made perfect in weakness."

2 Corinthians 12:9

In the fear of the LORD is strong confidence: and his children shall have a place of refuge.

Proverbs 14:26

Having therefore, brethren, boldness to enter into the holiest by the blood of Jesus, … Let us draw near with a true heart in full assurance of faith, having our hearts sprinkled from an evil conscience, and our bodies washed with pure water.

Hebrews 10:19, 22

The LORD is my light and my salvation; whom shall I fear? the LORD is the strength of my life; of whom shall I be afraid? … Though an host should encamp against me, my heart shall not fear: though war should rise against me, in this will I be confident.

Psalm 27:1, 3

GOD'S WORD OF LIFE ON
Self=Esteem

The LORD is my rock, and my fortress, and my deliverer; my God, my strength, in whom I will trust; my buckler, and the horn of my salvation, and my high tower. I will call upon the LORD, who is worthy to be praised: so shall I be saved from mine enemies.

Psalm 18:2–3

Blessed is the man that trusteth in the LORD, and whose hope the LORD is. For he shall be as a tree planted by the waters, and that spreadeth out her roots by the river, and shall not see when heat cometh, but her leaf shall be green; and shall not be careful in the year of drought, neither shall cease from yielding fruit.

Jeremiah 17:7–8

Thy hands have made me and fashioned me, LORD: give me understanding, that I may learn thy commandments.

Psalm 119:73

GOD'S WORDS OF LIFE ON
Self-Esteem

Beloved, if our heart condemn us not, then have we confidence toward God. And whatsoever we ask, we receive of him, because we keep his commandments, and do those things that are pleasing in his sight.

1 John 3:21–22

Thou wast precious in my sight, thou hast been honourable, and I have loved thee: therefore will I give men for thee, and people for thy life.

Isaiah 43:4

For thou hast possessed my reins: thou hast covered me in my mother's womb. I will praise thee; for I am fearfully and wonderfully made: marvellous are thy works; and that my soul knoweth right well.

Psalm 139:13–14

We may boldly say, The Lord is my helper, and I will not fear what man shall do unto me.

Hebrews 13:6

You Are Special!
Bishop Phillip H. Porter, Jr.

As a small child, I felt that greeting people was my *calling*. Even today, I find it comes naturally to greet people with a smile and nod as I walk down the street or into a restaurant.

You also have a *calling*—something that makes you special.

The Psalmist wrote these important words: "For thou hast possessed my reins: thou hast covered me in my mother's womb. I will praise thee; for I am fearfully and wonderfully made: marvellous are thy works; and that my soul knoweth right well" (Psalm 139:13–14).

Each of us has different life experiences. You may not have come from a nurturing home, but through the magnificent power of Jesus Christ, you can know that you are "fearfully and wonderfully made" by God for a unique and special purpose. Every human being was designed in their mother's womb by the hands of God. Shaped by the Lord himself, he has declared, "You are special!"

God giveth power to the faint; and to them that have no might he increaseth strength. Even the youths shall faint and be weary, and the young men shall utterly fall: But they that wait upon the LORD shall renew their strength; they shall mount up with wings as eagles; they shall run, and not be weary; and they shall walk, and not faint.

Isaiah 40:29–31

The Lord GOD will help me; therefore shall I not be confounded: therefore have I set my face like a flint, and I know that I shall not be ashamed.

Isaiah 50:7

Know I that the LORD saveth his anointed; he will hear him from his holy heaven with the saving strength of his right hand.

Psalm 20:6

Be strong and of a good courage, fear not, nor be afraid: ... for the LORD, thy God, he it is that doth go with thee; he will not fail thee, nor forsake thee.

Deuteronomy 31:6

GOD'S WORD OF LIFE ON
Strength

*God is our refuge and strength, a very present
help in trouble.*

Psalm 46:1

*Fear thou not; for I am with thee: be not dis-
mayed; for I am thy God: I will strengthen thee;
yea, I will help thee; yea, I will uphold thee with
the right hand of my righteousness.*

Isaiah 41:10

*I will love thee, O LORD, my strength. The LORD
is my rock, and my fortress, and my deliverer; my
God, my strength, in whom I will trust; my
buckler, and the horn of my salvation, and my
high tower.*

Psalm 18:1–2

*Blessed is the man whose strength is in thee, O
LORD; in whose heart are the ways of them.*

Psalm 84:5

*Be not afraid of sudden fear, neither of the desola-
tion of the wicked, when it cometh. For the LORD
shall be thy confidence, and shall keep thy foot
from being taken.*

Proverbs 3:25–26

God wilt light my candle: the LORD my God will enlighten my darkness. By thee I have run through a troop; and by my God have I leaped over a wall.

Psalm 18:28–29

O love the LORD, all ye his saints: for the LORD preserveth the faithful, and plentifully rewardeth the proud doer. Be of good courage, and he shall strengthen your heart, all ye that hope in the LORD.

Psalm 31:23–24

The LORD is my light and my salvation; whom shall I fear? The LORD is the strength of my life; of whom shall I be afraid? When the wicked, even mine enemies and my foes, came upon me to eat up my flesh, they stumbled and fell. Though an host should encamp against me, my heart shall not fear: though war should rise against me, in this will I be confident.

Psalm 27:1–3

God's Chosen Leader
Brother Matthew Parker

When Moses was asked by God to go to Pharaoh and bring the Israelites out of Egypt, he recognized his weakness. He asked, "Who am I?" God answered, "I AM WHO I AM." He wanted Moses to know that it didn't matter how weak he was—only how strong God is!

The African-American community has had many leaders: Richard Allen, Frederick Douglas, Harriet Tubman, Sojourner Truth, Mary Bethune, Booker T. Washington, W. E. B. DuBois, Martin Luther King, Jr., and others, who, like Moses, were raised up from humble beginnings and used to bring liberation and salvation to our people. We have witnessed how "God hath chosen the weak things of the world to confound the things which are mighty" (1 Corinthians 1:27).

Even now, God is looking for people like you and me to bring deliverance, liberation, and salvation to African-American people. We go with Christ's words to Paul: "My grace is sufficient for thee: for my strength is made perfect in weakness" (2 Corinthians 12:9).

Humility and the fear of the LORD are riches, and honour, and life.

Proverbs 22:4

Blessed is the man that walketh not in the counsel of the ungodly, nor standeth in the way of sinners, nor sitteth in the seat of the scornful. But his delight is in the law of the LORD; and in his law doth he meditate day and night. And he shall be like a tree planted by the rivers of water, that bringeth forth his fruit in his season; his leaf also shall not wither; and whatsoever he doeth shall prosper.

Psalm 1:1–3

[Wisdom spoke]: "Riches and honour are with me; yea, durable riches and righteousness. My fruit is better than gold, yea, than fine gold; and my revenue than choice silver. I lead in the way of righteousness, in the midst of the paths of judgment: That I may cause those that love me to inherit substance; and I will fill their treasures."

Proverbs 8:18–21

It shall come to pass, if thou shalt hearken diligently unto the voice of the LORD thy God, to observe and to do all his commandments which I command thee this day, that the LORD thy God will set thee on high above all nations of the earth: And all these blessings shall come on thee, and overtake thee, if thou shalt hearken unto the voice of the LORD thy God. ... The LORD shall command the blessing upon thee in thy storehouses, and in all that thou settest thine hand unto; and he shall bless thee in the land which the LORD thy God giveth thee.

Deuteronomy 28:1–2, 8

This book of the law shall not depart out of thy mouth; but thou shalt meditate therein day and night, that thou mayest observe to do according to all that is written therein: for then thou shalt make thy way prosperous, and then thou shalt have good success.

Joshua 1:8

*Let them shout for joy, and be glad, that favour
my righteous cause: yea, let them say continually,
Let the LORD be magnified, which hath pleasure
in the prosperity of his servant.*

Psalm 35:27

*Believe in the LORD your God, so shall ye be
established; believe his prophets, so shall ye
prosper.*

2 Chronicles 20:20

*He that covereth his sins shall not prosper: but
whoso confesseth and forsaketh them shall
have mercy.*

Proverbs 28:13

*He becometh poor that dealeth with a slack hand:
but the hand of the diligent maketh rich.*

Proverbs 10:4

*The LORD hear thee in the day of trouble; the
name of the God of Jacob defend thee; … Grant
thee according to thine own heart, and fulfil all
thy counsel.*

Psalm 20:1, 4

Success

Without counsel purposes are disappointed: but in the multitude of counsellors they are established.

Proverbs 15:22

Promotion cometh neither from the east, nor from the west, nor from the south. But God is the judge: he putteth down one, and setteth up another.

Psalm 75:6–7

Commit thy works unto the LORD, and thy thoughts shall be established.

Proverbs 16:3

A bruised reed shall God not break, and smoking flax shall he not quench, till he send forth judgment unto victory.

Matthew 12:20

O sing unto the LORD a new song; for he hath done marvelous things: his right hand, and his holy arm, hath gotten him the victory.

Psalm 98:1

Whatsoever is born of God overcometh the world: and this is the victory that overcometh the world, even our faith. Who is he that overcometh the world, but he that believeth that Jesus is the Son of God?

1 John 5:4–5

In a moment, in the twinkling of an eye, at the last trump: for the trumpet shall sound, and the dead shall be raised incorruptible, and we shall be changed. ... So when this corruptible shall have put on incorruption, and this mortal shall have put on immortality, then shall be brought to pass the saying that is written, Death is swallowed up in victory. O death, where is thy sting? O grave, where is thy victory? The sting of death is sin; and the strength of sin is the law. But thanks be to God, which giveth the victory through our Lord Jesus Christ.

1 Corinthians 15:52, 54–57

Remember Your Dreams
Dr. Bennett W. Smith, Sr.

The account of Joseph as he struggled against hardship, accusations, and incarceration should be read to all the hopeless, the least, the lost, and the left out. For in his story, we see that God honored Joseph's great dreams and visions of success.

The Bible makes no mention of Joseph's dreams after he arrived in Egypt. They seem to have faded away completely. This is the case with many oppressed people. Their dreams seem to be only fantasies they lose when they wake in the morning. The pain and hardship of their present realities—inflamed by educational, cultural, social, racial, and gender structures—suppress their dreams of successful accomplishments.

But Joseph's story reminds us that no matter how faded our dreams may become, God manifests his presence and power in the realm of time to those of childlike faith. Just as he did with Joseph, God does, in his own time and in his own way, make dreams come true. Remember your dreams.

GOD'S WORDS OF LIFE ON
Thankfulness

God hast turned for me my mourning into dancing: God hast put off my sackcloth, and girded me with gladness; To the end that my glory may sing praise to him, and not be silent. O LORD my God, I will give thanks unto thee for ever.

Psalm 30:11–12

In every thing give thanks: for this is the will of God in Christ Jesus concerning you.

1 Thessalonians 5:18

I exhort ... that, first of all, supplications, prayers, intercessions, and giving of thanks, be made for all men; for kings, and for all that are in authority; that we may lead a quiet and peaceable life in all godliness and honesty. For this is good and acceptable in the sight of God our Saviour.

1 Timothy 2:1–3

Thanks be to God, which giveth us the victory through our Lord Jesus Christ.

1 Corinthians 15:57

O give thanks unto the LORD; for he is good; for his mercy endureth for ever. O give thanks unto the God of gods, for his mercy endureth for ever. O give thanks to the Lord of lords: for his mercy endureth for ever.

Psalm 136:1–3

[Give] thanks unto the Father, which hath made us meet to be partakers of the inheritance of the saints in light: Who hath delivered us from the power of darkness, and hath translated us into the kingdom of his dear Son: In whom we have redemption through his blood, even the forgiveness of sins.

Colossians 1:12–14

I will praise the name of God with a song, and will magnify him with thanksgiving. This also shall please the LORD better than an ox or bullock that hath horns and hoofs. The humble shall see this, and be glad: and your heart shall live that seek God.

Psalm 69:30–32

GOD'S WORDS OF LIFE ON
Thankfulness

*Let us come before God's presence with thanks-
giving, and make a joyful noise unto him with
psalms. ... For he is our God; and we are the people of his pasture, and the sheep of his hand.*

Psalm 95:2, 7

*I will mention the lovingkindnesses of the LORD,
and the praises of the LORD, according to all that
the LORD hath bestowed on us, and the great
goodness toward the house of Israel, which he
hath bestowed on them according to his mercies,
and according to the multitude of his lovingkindnesses. For he said, Surely they are my people,
children that will not lie: so he was their Savior.*

Isaiah 63:7–8

*I cease not to give thanks for you, making men-
tion of you in my prayers; That the God of our
Lord Jesus Christ, the Father of glory, may give
unto you the spirit of wisdom and revelation in
the knowledge of him.*

Ephesians 1:16–17

We are bound to give thanks always to God for you, brethren beloved of the Lord, because God hath from the beginning chosen you to salvation through sanctification of the Spirit and belief of the truth; Whereunto he called you by our gospel, to the obtaining of the glory of our Lord Jesus Christ.

2 Thessalonians 2:13–14

Enter into God's gates with thanksgiving, and into his courts with praise: be thankful unto him, and bless his name. For the LORD is good; his mercy is everlasting; and his truth endureth to all generations.

Psalm 100:4–5

Every creature of God is good, and nothing to be refused, if it be received with thanksgiving: For it is sanctified by the word of God and prayer.

1 Timothy 4:4–5

Thanks be unto God, which always causeth us to triumph in Christ, and makest manifest the savour of his knowledge by us in every place.

2 Corinthians 2:14

GOD'S WORDS OF LIFE ON
Thankfulness

*As ye have therefore received Christ Jesus the
Lord, so walk ye in him: Rooted and built up in
him, and stablished in the faith, as ye have been
taught, abounding therein with thanksgiving.*

Colossians 2: 6–7

*Blessing, and glory, and wisdom, and thanksgiv-
ing, and honour, and power, and might, be unto
our God for ever and ever. Amen.*

Revelation 7:12

*By Christ therefore let us offer the sacrifice of
praise to God continually, that is, the fruit of our
lips giving thanks to his name. To do good and
communicate forget not: for with such sacrifices
God is well pleased.*

Hebrews 13:15–16

*Let your moderation be known unto all men.
The Lord is at hand. Be careful for nothing; but
in every thing by prayer and supplication with
thanksgiving let your requests be made known
unto God. And the peace of God, which passeth
all understanding, shall keep your hearts and
minds through Christ Jesus.*

Philippians 4:5–7

Giving Thanks
Dr. Rudolph W. McKissick, Jr.

As African Americans, God has richly blessed us. We know that our lives here may not be perfect (from our perspective), but we must look at the blessings we have from God. We must acknowledge that we have moved from poverty to owning banks; from illiteracy to founding educational institutions; from slave quarters to home ownership.

We know that God is the source of everything we have. Therefore, it is incumbent on us to practice proper stewardship. Like David, we should give back to God out of thanksgiving for what he has given us, recognizing that it all belongs to him. This involves more than our tithes and offerings, but encompasses every area of life in which we have experienced God's blessings.

In our homes, on our jobs, in our places of worship, and in our living, we praise God for all he has given us, not simply by telling him "Thank you," but by using it for his purposes.

Jesus said, "Thou sayest that I am a king. To this end was I born, and for this cause came I into the world, that I should bear witness unto the truth. Every one that is of the truth heareth my voice."

John 18:37

We know that the Son of God is come, and hath given us an understanding, that we may know him that is true, and we are in him that is true, even in his Son Jesus Christ. This is the true God, and eternal life.

1 John 5:20

LORD, who shall abide in thy tabernacle? who shall dwell in thy holy hill? He that walketh uprightly, and worketh righteousness, and speaketh the truth in his heart.

Psalm 15:1–2

The LORD is nigh unto all them that call upon him, to all that call upon him in truth.

Psalm 145:18

He that speaketh truth showeth forth righteousness.

Proverbs 12:17

GOD'S WORD OF LIFE ON
Truth

Jesus said, "I am the way, the truth, and the life: no man cometh unto the Father, but by me."

John 14:6

Thy word is true from the beginning, O LORD: and every one of thy righteous judgments endureth for ever.

Psalm 119:160

He that walketh righteously, and speaketh uprightly; he that despiseth the gain of oppressions, that shaketh his hands from holding of bribes, that stoppeth his ears from hearing of blood, and shutteth his eyes from seeing evil; He shall dwell on high: his place of defence shall be the munitions of rocks: bread shall be given him; his waters shall be sure.

Isaiah 33:15–16

The word of the LORD is right; and all his works are done in truth. He loveth righteousness and judgment: the earth is full of the goodness of the LORD.

Psalm 33:4–5

A true witness delivereth souls.

Proverbs 14:25

*The fear of the LORD is clean, enduring for ever:
the judgments of the LORD are true and righteous
altogether. More to be desired are they than gold,
yea, than much fine gold: sweeter also than honey
and the honeycomb.*

Psalm 19:9–10

*Lying lips are abomination to the LORD: but they
that deal truly are his delight.*

Proverbs 12:22

*Brethren, whatsoever things are true, whatsoever
things are honest, whatsoever things are just,
whatsoever things are pure, whatsoever things are
lovely, whatsoever things are of good report; if
there be any virtue, and if there be any praise,
think on these things. Those things, which ye have
both learned, and received, and heard, and seen in
me, do: and the God of peace shall be with you.*

Philippians 4:8–9

GOD'S WORD OF LIFE ON
Truth

*The LORD is the true God, he is the living God,
and an everlasting king.*

Jeremiah 10:10

*Thou, O LORD, art a God full of compassion, and
gracious, longsuffering, and plenteous in mercy
and truth.*

Psalm 86:15

*When much people were gathered together, and
were come to Jesus out of every city, he spake by a
parable: A sower went out to sow his seed: and as
he sowed, some fell by the way side; ... And other
fell on good ground, and sprang up, and bare fruit
an hundredfold. ... Now the parable is this: The
seed is the word of God. ... That on the good
ground are they, which in an honest and good
heart, having heard the word, keep it, and bring
forth fruit with patience.*

Luke 8:4–5, 8, 11, 15

*The words of wise men are heard in quiet more
than the cry of him that ruleth among fools.*

Ecclesiastes 9:17

GOD'S WORDS OF LIFE ON
Truth

Ye shall know the truth, and the truth shall make you free.

John 8:32

Pleasant words are as an honeycomb, sweet to the soul, and health to the bones.

Proverbs 16:24

If any man speak, let him speak as the oracles of God; if any man minister, let him do it as of the ability which God giveth: that God in all things may be glorified through Jesus Christ, to whom be praise and dominion for ever and ever.

1 Peter 4:11

Speaking the truth in love, … grow up into him in all things, which is the head, even Christ.

Ephesians 4:15

Jesus said, "Howbeit when he, the Spirit of truth is come, he will guide you into all truth: for he shall not speak of himself; but whatsoever he shall hear, that shall he speak: and he will show you things to come.

John 16:13

Walking in God's Truth

Reverend Dr. Suzan Johnson Cook

Today we need men and women who will unashamedly walk in truth. Though it seems to have become popular and even permissible to tell "little lies," talk back, curse, be sore losers at sports events, and to walk "out of the truth," we need those among us who heed Paul's word to the early Christians to "stand therefore, having your loins gird about with truth, and having on the breastplate of righteousness" (Ephesians 6:14).

Christians must stand tall—even if it means standing alone—in the truth. My parents used to say, "Our word is our bond," and "We must live life so that others can trust us to do that which we say we will do."

So go forward, my brothers and sisters! Walk in truth—just as Nelson Mandela walked to his freedom and Harriet Tubman walked to her freedom. Do not look back into the darkness, but look forward to the light of truth at the end of the dark tunnel.

GOD'S WORDS OF LIFE ON
Wisdom

Happy is the man that findeth wisdom, and the man that getteth understanding. For the merchandise of it is better than the merchandise of silver, and the gain thereof than fine gold.
Proverbs 3:13–14

If any of you lack wisdom, let him ask of God, that giveth to all men liberally, and upbraideth not; and it shall be given him.
James 1:5

Wisdom is the principal thing; therefore get wisdom: and with all thy getting get understanding. Exalt her, and she shall promote thee: she shall bring thee to honour, when thou dost embrace her.
Proverbs 4:7–8

When wisdom entereth into thine heart, and knowledge is pleasant unto thy soul; Discretion shall preserve thee, understanding shall keep thee.
Proverbs 2:10–11

So shall the knowledge of wisdom be unto thy soul: when thou hast found it, then there shall be a reward, and thy expectation shall not be cut off.
Proverbs 24:14

GOD'S WORD OF LIFE ON
Wisdom

Wisdom strengtheneth the wise more than ten mighty men which are in the city.

Ecclesiastes 7:19

Teach us to number our days, that we may apply our hearts unto wisdom.

Psalm 90:12

Now we have received, not the spirit of the world, but the spirit which is of God; that we might know the things that are freely given to us of God. Which things also we speak, not in the words which man's wisdom teacheth, but which the Holy Ghost teacheth; comparing spiritual things with spiritual. The natural man receiveth not the things of the Spirit of God: for they are foolishness unto him: neither can he know them, because they are spiritually discerned. But he that is spiritual judgeth all things, yet he himself is judged of no man. For who hath known the mind of the Lord, that he may instruct him? But we have the mind of Christ.

1 Corinthians 2:12–16

God's Words of Life on
Wisdom

The LORD giveth wisdom: out of his mouth cometh knowledge and understanding. He layeth up sound wisdom for the righteous.

Proverbs 2:6–7

The fear of the LORD is the beginning of wisdom: a good understanding have all they that do his commandments: his praise endureth for ever.

Psalm 111:10

Thine ears shall hear a word behind thee, saying, This is the way, walk ye in it, when ye turn to the right hand, and when ye turn to the left.

Isaiah 30:21

He that getteth wisdom loveth his own soul: he that keepeth understanding shall find good.

Proverbs 19:8

The wisdom that is from above is first pure, then peaceable, gentle, and easy to be entreated, full of mercy and good fruits, without partiality, and without hypocrisy. And the fruit of righteousness is sown in peace of them that make peace.

James 3:17–18

GOD'S WORD OF LIFE ON
Wisdom

Wisdom is good with an inheritance: and by it there is profit to them that see the sun. For wisdom is a defence, and money is a defence: but the excellency of knowledge is, that wisdom giveth life to them that have it.

Ecclesiastes 7:11–12

Behold, God desireth truth in the inward parts: and in the hidden part God shall make me to know wisdom.

Psalm 51:6

Who is as the wise man? and who knoweth the interpretation of a thing? a man's wisdom maketh his face to shine, and the boldness of his face shall be changed.

Ecclesiastes 8:1

Whence then cometh wisdom? and where is the place of understanding? Seeing it is hid from the eyes of all living, and kept close from the fowls of the air. God understandeth the way thereof, and he knoweth the place thereof.

Job 28:20–21, 23

GOD'S WORDS OF LIFE ON
Wisdom

Hear ... and receive my sayings; and the years of thy life shall be many. I have taught thee in the way of wisdom; I have led thee in right paths. When thou goest, thy steps shall not be straitened; and when thou runnest, thou shalt not stumble. Take fast hold of instruction; let her not go: keep her; for she is thy life.

Proverbs 4:10–13

Be strong in the grace that is in Christ Jesus. And the things that thou hast heard of me among many witnesses, the same commit thou to faithful men, who shall be able to teach others also. ... Consider what I say; and the Lord give thee understanding in all things.

2 Timothy 2:1–2, 7

Whoso keepeth the commandment shall feel no evil thing: and a wise man's heart discerneth both time and judgment.

Ecclesiastes 8:5

"Don't Go There!"
Reverend Dr. Alicia D. Byrd

Don't go there!" is an expression used by young people to warn others when they're about to say or do something that has undesirable consequences. Can't you just hear God saying, "Don't go there!" when Satan told Adam and Eve to eat of the tree of the knowledge of good and evil? Satan started with innuendo: "Did God say that?" He appealed to their intelligence: "Who do you know that died from eating the fruit of a tree?" He closed with an appeal to ego: "There's nothing wrong with being on God's level."

Each time, God tried to tell Adam and Eve: "Don't listen! This advice is wrong. Don't go there!" But instead of listening to God, Adam and Eve "went there" anyway—with devastating results.

Even though we might not see or understand the reason behind God's wisdom and counsel, it's better to obey. His wisdom will always bring us health and peace, and keep us out of destructive entanglements.

GOD'S WORDS OF LIFE ON
Work

Whatsoever ye do, do it heartily, as to the Lord,
and not unto men; Knowing that of the Lord ye
shall receive the reward of the inheritance: for ye
serve the Lord Christ.

Colossians 3:23–24

He that doeth the will of God abideth for ever.

1 John 2:17

It is good and comely for one to eat and to drink,
and to enjoy the good of all his labour that he
taketh under the sun all the days of his life, which
God giveth him: for it is his portion. Every man
also to whom God hath given riches and wealth,
and hath given him power to eat thereof, and to
take his portion, and to rejoice in his labour; this
is the gift of God.

Ecclesiastes 5:18–19

He becometh poor that dealeth with a slack hand:
but the hand of the diligent maketh rich.

Proverbs 10:4

GOD'S WORD OF LIFE ON
Work

Therefore, my beloved brethren, be ye stedfast, unmoveable, always abounding in the work of the Lord, forasmuch as ye know that your labour is not in vain in the Lord.

1 Corinthians 15:58

Unto thee, O LORD, belongeth mercy: for thou renderest to every man according to his work.

Psalm 62:12

Jesus said, "Labour not for the meat which perisheth, but for that meat which endureth unto everlasting life, which the Son of man shall give unto you."

John 6:27

Be ye strong, ... and let not your hands be weak: for your work shall be rewarded.

2 Chronicles 15:7

Jesus said, "Come unto me, all ye that labour and are heavy laden, and I will give you rest."

Matthew 11:28

GOD'S WORDS OF LIFE ON
Work

Let thy work appear unto thy servants, and thy glory unto their children. And let the beauty of the LORD our God be upon us: and establish thou the work of our hands upon us; yea, the work of our hands establish thou it.

Psalm 90:16–17

Walk worthy of the Lord unto all pleasing, being fruitful in every good work, and increasing in the knowledge of God; Strengthened with all might, according to his glorious power, unto all patience and longsuffering with joyfulness.

Colossians 1:10–11

O love the LORD, all ye his saints: for the LORD preserveth the faithful, and plentifully rewardeth the proud doer.

Psalm 31:23

I the LORD search the heart, I try the reins, even to give every man according to his ways, and according to the fruit of his doings.

Jeremiah 17:10

*According to the grace of God which is given
unto me, as a wise masterbuilder, I have laid the
foundation, and another buildeth theron. But let
every man take heed how he buildeth thereupon.
For other foundation can no man lay than that is
laid, which is Jesus Christ. Now if any man build
upon this foundation gold, silver, precious stones,
wood, hay, stubble; Every man's work shall be
made manifest: for the day shall declare it,
because it shall be revealed by fire; and the fire
shall try every man's work of what sort it is. If any
man's work abide which he hath built thereupon,
he shall receive a reward.*

1 Corinthians 3:10–14

*Not by works of righteousness which we have
done, but according to God's mercy he saved us,
by the washing of regeneration, and renewing of
the Holy Ghost.*

Titus 3:5

GOD'S WORDS OF LIFE ON
Work

God is not unrighteous to forget your work and labour of love, which ye have showed toward his name, in that ye have ministered to the saints, and do minister.

Hebrews 6:10

God is able to make all grace abound toward you; that ye, always having all sufficiency in all things, may abound to every good work.

2 Corinthians 9:8

This book of the law shall not depart out of thy mouth; but thou shalt meditate therein day and night, that thou mayest observe to do according to all that is written therein: for then thou shalt make thy way prosperous, and then thou shalt have good success.

Joshua 1:8

[God's people] ... shall long enjoy the work of their hands. They shall not labour in vain, nor bring forth for trouble; for they are the seed of the blessed of the LORD, and their offspring with them.

Isaiah 65:22–23

Too Busy to be Trifling

Dr. Willie T. Snead

Sometimes people with great aspirations are targeted by those who attempt little and achieve minimally. Instead of rising to the level of great achievers, many are content to live well below their ability, pulling others down instead of pushing them toward success.

Sanballot and Geshem tried to distract Nehemiah as he supervised the rebuilding of the walls around the city of Jerusalem. But Nehemiah refused to fall for their foolishness. He left a message for those of all ages who dare to complete their work in spite of detractors: "I am doing a great work, that I cannot come down" (Nehemiah 6:3).

When others seek to divert your attention from excellence and achievement in pastoral work, academics, family relationships, and professional work with petty distractions, let them know you cannot be deflected from God's work. God has given you a job to do and you cannot stop until the work is done.